DARK SPACE

DARK SPACE

ARCHITECTURE
REPRESENTATION
BLACK IDENTITY

MARIO GOODEN

COLUMBIA BOOKS ON
ARCHITECTURE AND THE CITY

CONTENTS

"MADE IN AMERICA": THERE IS NO SUCH THING AS AFRICAN AMERICAN ARCHITECTURE

Most African Americans, if given a chance, would have chosen to be "just Americans" ever since the first of us was brought here to Jamestown colony in 1619, a year before the Mayflower landed. But that choice has never been left up to us.[1]

–Clarence Page, columnist for the *Chicago Tribune*, 1996

In the December 19, 1991 OpEd pages of the *Washington Post*, the conservative commentator, columnist, and baseball enthusiast George F. Will penned a not-so-innocent commentary, titled "Homespun Sport," about the history of the game of basketball on the 100th anniversary of its birth. The author of such sporting titles as *Men at Work: The Craft of Baseball and Bunts* begins his piece with a nostalgic description of a small wooden relic–a piece of the floor of the old gym in Springfield, Massachusetts where, in the winter of 1891, Dr. James Naismith invented the game of basketball. Then thirty years old and in charge of physical education instruction at the International YMCA, Naismith was struck by the relative lack of sports that could be played during the region's harsh winters. The original baskets were just that–two peach baskets hung from the lower rail of the gym's balcony, which was exactly 10 feet high. "Just as the Civil War spread baseball across the country like butter over bread," Will writes, "young YMCA administrators carried the gospel of basketball."[2] After this apparently straightforward introduction, a subtle hinge develops in the text. While keeping his pivot-foot in place, Will states:

> Basketball has two archetypes–the small-town midwestern white kid with a crew cut and jump shot, and the black kid in the city, playing the game of inexpensive equipment and confined spaces. Basketball in its early urban incarnations was considered a Jewish game. Then some other of society's outsiders got inside, and the game was transformed.[3]

Here, Will gets off a jump shot that I must admit I had not seen coming. In this last sentence, Will acknowledges the existence of racial and colonial "others"–a fundamental condition of the American experience–while simultaneously initiating a process of "de-othering" black identity.

The essay then proceeds to mention that many of the achievements of blacks along the march toward inclusion in American society involved athletics. These milestones included the March 19, 1966 NCAA basketball championship game in College Park, Maryland, where the University of Texas at El Paso (then Texas Western College) beat the University of Kentucky, 72-65. At the time, there were no black players on any of the teams of the ACC (Atlantic Coast Conference), the SWC (Southwest Conference), or the SEC (Southeast Conference), the last of which included Kentucky. Adolph Rupp—then head coach at the University of Kentucky, whose name now graces Kentucky's Rupp Arena—was among those who steadfastly resisted the integration of the sport. Angered at being pressured by the University of Kentucky's president to recruit minority players in 1966, Rupp yelled at an assistant: "That sonofabitch is ordering me to get some niggers in here. What am I going to do?"[4] His team's loss to Texas Western (TWC) in the NCAA finals made him still further indignant, as TWC was a team that started five black players (and played only two substitutes, both of whom were black). This was a first for an NCAA championship game. Rupp would later comment, "TWC… TWC? What's that stand for—Two White Coaches?"[5]

In a construction of relationships between distinct American cultural forms (baseball, basketball, and jazz) George Will argues that basketball is the most purely American game because it has no evolutionary connections, as baseball and football do, with other nations' games. As such, it has become a showcase for black talent—as it should be, in Will's reading, because blacks are "the most purely American Americans." With subtle irony, he substitutes "American American" for the expected label "African American." In doing this, Will eliminates the double-consciousness of black identity as well as the signifier of always seeing oneself through the gaze of a white lens. This twist by the conservative columnist propels us toward the center of discussions regarding culture and cultural productions for blacks in America, a collective whose history has long been fraught with pressure for the black American—in the words of W.E.B. Du Bois—"to be both a Negro and an American, without being cursed and spit upon by his fellows, without having the doors of Opportunity closed roughly in his face."[6] Yet, any investigation of issues of culture and race must recognize that culture operates within the parameters of historical and social contexts. Furthermore, historical and social contexts are inseparable from geography and time, which means that the definition of culture is tantamount to comprehending one's relationship to a particular place in time. Hence, culture cannot be essentialized to ethnic identity.

Culture is an understanding of one's internal and external relationships to place (geography) and time (the order in which events occur), as well as an intimacy with one's own existence (the materiality of presence and self). According to Georg Simmel, culture comes into being through the synthesis of the subjective spirit and the objective intellectual product.[7] However, unlike sports, music, film, art, and design—which are cultural productions defined by representation, patterns of consumption, and in some cases mass production—architecture is neither consumed nor indiscrimantly mass produced. Architecture spatializes political, social, and historical relationships as well as instrumentalizes subjectivities. It brackets place, time, and materiality to events in order to produce meanings and discourse. Therefore, architecture can neither be essentialized to race nor racial representations—a process that invariably results in stereotypes, commodification of identity, and a regime of visibility that reifies the dichotomies of otherness (white versus black, us versus them) in American discourse.

George Will concludes his column with a quote from Du Bois:

> Once for all, let us realize that we are Americans, that we were brought here with the earliest settlers and that the very sort of civilization from which we came made the complete absorption of Western modes and customs imperative if we were to survive at all; in brief, there is nothing so indigenous, so completely "made in America," as we.[8]

When African slaves arrived in the American colonies, they were deprived of the cultural artifacts that had identified them in their homelands. They were stripped from their homelands, stripped from their families, stripped from their cultural traditions, stripped from their traditional dress, and sold bare upon the auction blocks of colonial slave markets. African slaves were even stripped of their names and given new names by slaveowners. All visual motifs of identity were stripped as well. Among certain ethnic groups in Africa, one's body was marked or face scarred with certain symbols that mapped that individual's position and identity within the social geography of the group. This was a common practice among the ancient kingdoms of West Africa, such as the Kingdoms of Ghana, Mali, and Songhai, and the practice continues today among certain peoples of Nigeria (a terrain inclusive of over 250 different ethnic groups) as an indication of one's cultural heritage. Three scars on the left and right cheeks of a man or woman reveal that that person is a descendant of a slave tribe or class. Such customs were suppressed on American soil, and there is no evidence of those practices today among descendents of African slaves.

Yet, while the overt visual symbols and motifs disappeared, intangible traces of identity remained among Americans of African decent. These intangible traces enabled the forging of a new identity, of which American slaves are the ancestral authors and contemporary black Americans are the inheritors. If the tribal markings of ancient kingdoms have disappeared, they have been replaced by indelible markers of American identity in terms of body language, gestures, postures, and movement. The slave body, which originally belonged not to the black American but to the slaveowner, has become, for black Americans, an instrument of social and political commentary and protest, in subtle, elusive, and ambiguous ways. "Black Style," as it has been called, involves an "evolving semiotics of black self-creation that has been designed from its very outset to impose a degree of individuality on the numbing uniformity bred of slavery, poverty, Jim Crow laws, and white racism." According to Shane White and Graham White in *African American Expressive Culture from Its Beginnings to the Zoot Suit*, the politics of "Black Style"—not only its body language and gestures, but also its hairstyles, clothing, and dance moves—are the politics of metaphor. It is a politics that is always ambiguous, yet meant to act subtly against the dominant racial group.[9] However, this politics is not as simple as wearing an Afro, a dashiki, or other afro-centric fashions. In fact, it is not a politics of style that refers to images and representations at all. Rather, it is a politics that refers to spatial praxes and resistance. This is the manner in which blacks occupy and move through space, negotiate spatial relationships, and create alternative spaces for creative expression and daily affirmation of life in American society.

I recall walking down the street alone in the middle of a very hot November day in the Malian capital city of Bamako several years ago when a teenage Malian boy yelled at me from across the street, "Hey! American guy." I turned and looked around to figure out to whom he was speaking, and when I saw that I was alone on this part of the street, I realized that he was speaking to me. I must admit that I had never really thought of myself as being identifiably American. Perhaps a bit pretentiously, I had always simply considered myself a citizen of the world. And I was surprised that as a dark-skinned man walking in West Africa, in plain clothes without some

American slogan or identifiable fashion label across my chest, I could be recognized immediately as American. I wondered, and still wonder to this day—what gave me away?

Within modern cultural production, these aforementioned intangible traits of manner and space-making influenced and in some cases transformed modern dance, music, and visual arts. Although racism was pervasive in the modern dance world in the 1940s and 1950s, the inclusion of black dancers in the Martha Graham Dance Company, and especially the participation of Alvin Ailey and Carmen de Lavallade in the Lester Horton Dancers, led to the development of what is now considered American jazz dance. Alvin Ailey extended Horton's legacy and founded the American Dance Theater following Horton's death in 1953, including many of the former members of Horton's company. The American Dance Theater later became the Alvin Ailey Dance Company. Katherine Dunham—a dancer, choreographer, and anthropologist—directed the Katherine Dunham Troupe and combined African and Caribbean movements, in the process revolutionizing American dance by understanding from an anthropological point of view the roots of black dance, ritual, and spatial movement, and by transforming them into a significant artistic choreography that speaks to audiences regardless of race.

In music, these intangible traces ignited the passions of the blues, whose meters and cadences measured not only the despair of blacks but the triumph of the black spirit. And of course jazz—"America's classical music," with a history much too well known and complex to recite here—is the first indigenous American style to affect music in the rest of the world. From ragtime syncopation and driving brass bands to soaring gospel choirs, field hollers, and the deep down growl of the blues, jazz's many roots are celebrated almost everywhere in the United States. Its rhythms and improvisations are a direct reflection of black spatial relationships to society, culture, and politics. Likewise in the visual arts, the paintings of Jacob Lawrence and the collages of Romare Beardon capture the motion, history, and complexities of black American life. The vivid yet abstract black bodies in Lawrence's works (such as the sixty panel *Migration Series,* which depicts the Great Migration of black Americans from the rural South to the urban North) are set in motion relative to each other and relative to their historical and social contexts. Further, Beardon's collage-like process of layered fragments of colored paper and cut-outs from magazines creates complex spatial relationships of simultaneity, movement, and overlaps of visual foregrounds and cultural backgrounds.

These examples escape the traps of essentialism and stereotypes, and suggest that black identity is neither determined by the color of Lawrence's or Beardon's abstract figures, nor by the costumes of Ailey's dancer, nor the skin color of the jazz performer. Rather, black identity is wrapped up in the spatial expression of the black experience that is translated through these modes of productions. How can *architectural* modes of production, then, resist image and representation to translate the black American experience into spatial forms, and to create alternative spaces for creative expression and affirmation of daily life in American society? How can architecture synthesize the subjective spirit and the objective intellectual product to construct a uniquely "American American" architecture borne of black complexity?

Yet the absorption of black cultural production into the larger category of "Made in America" in fact began with the initial introduction of African slaves to the American continent in ways that are not limited to slave labor. This absorption takes the form not only of subtle cultural traces, but includes direct slave knowledge. Noted historian Robert Rosen chronicled the introduction of rice production in the Carolinas during the seventeenth century in *A Short History of Charleston*. European settlers had little knowledge of how to cultivate rice, since it had not been grown in northern Europe or England. Slave traders and Englishmen noted that rice "forms the chief part of the African's sustenance" and was abundant on the "Windward Coast" of Africa, an area now known as Ghana. According to Rosen, "the planters obviously knew the value of slaves who knew how to cultivate rice because advertisements for slaves often indicated their origin. One advertisement, for example, read 'from the Windward Rice Coast.'" Hence, black slaves probably taught white planters how to cultivate it since Africans had been cultivating it for centuries. The rice planters of Carolina grew so rich that they became the wealthiest people in the American colonies.[10]

James Draper examines the many theories regarding African contributions to architecture in the United States in an essay titled "From Slave Cabins to 'Shotguns': Perceptions on Africanisms in American Architecture":

> With the emergence of the new social history during the
> 1960s, came more inclusive and objective studies into
> the vernacular architecture of African Americans and the re-
> formulation of earlier ethnocentric interpretations. This can
> be observed in the recent illuminations on the shotgun house
> and how it has become not only an important artifact in the
> study of African-American history, but how it has also become
> a symbol of the retention of African traditional social and cul-
> tural traits within the United States.[11]

Furthermore, historian John Michael Vlach identifies the "shotgun house" (a narrow rectangular house no more than twelve feet wide with rooms arranged as an *enfilade* and doors at each end of the house) as a continuation of an African lifestyle. According to Vlach, the ninety degree rotation of the house from conventional American folk housing is a "formal index of an alternative architectural tradition."[12]

While historians have primarily focused on the tectonics and formal attributes of domestic structures of slaves, and the vernacular structures of black Americans have only recently gained attention, the spatial praxis of these environments holds clearer evidence of the cultural transference from Africa to America. The architect Laverne Wells-Bowie and noted cultural theoretician bell hooks explore black cultural connections to space in *Art on My Mind: Visual Politics*. Wells-Bowie's research has examined Gullah architecture and what she calls a "deep structure" in the ways in which all areas of the African Diaspora use and shape space. (Gullah refers to the culture and language that developed in the slave communities of the isolated plantations along coastal South Carolina and Georgia. The Gullah language is a Creole blend of Elizabethan English and African languages, and is still spoken today among the people of John's Island, South Carolina.) Wells-Bowie and hooks discuss the extension of interior domestic spaces to the exterior space of the yard, and the domestic territorialization of that space to accommodate communal space and domestic rituals like "sweeping the yard." The fashioning of the yard was and is as crucial as the fashioning of the interior environment.[13] Furthermore, the hand-built vernacular houses of poor Southern blacks exhibit resistance to oppression in the manner by which blacks could have the right to exercise control over space on their own terms—and where imagination and design "would respond to the needs of their lives, their communities, their families." hooks writes, "No matter how poor you were in the shack, no matter if you owned the shack or not, there you could allow your needs and desires to articulate interior design and exterior surroundings."[14]

Furthermore, black domestic life and labor gave rise to a significant number of inventions borne of arduous tasks and limited resources. These inventions have been absorbed into the broader definition of "Made in America" and are now taken for granted and rarely credited to their black makers. Although the list is too exhaustive to recount, Mitchell Brown's *Index of African American Inventors* provides a remarkable look at the scope of industrial and domestic ingenuity that came out of the work of black Americans (including biscuit cutters, folding beds, rotary engines, street sweepers, railway signals, corn and cotton planting devices, ironing boards, lawnmowers, umbrella stands, a carpet beating machine, an automatic fishing device, ice-cream molds, photo embossing, refrigeration apparatuses, variations on the guitar, the golf tee, pencil sharpeners, electromechanical brakes, and a design for an airship).[15] These are inventions that have had significant impacts on the development of American architecture, landscape, and space.

This book returns to the question of architecture and black culture, an interplay that is perhaps caught between the indelible traces of identity and the absorption of spatial and cultural practices into a dominant culture. This intersection of architecture and black American life does not simply express the static conditions of ethnic identity. Rather, as a cultural practice, architecture must interpret and translate the historical, social, and political contexts of a place and how one comes to terms with that place. Such an architecture should reveal meanings, situations, and conditions (both apparent and subliminal) and allow for individual participatory action, the affirmation of "presence" in life, and a recognition of existential meaning and knowledge—the confirmation of that life, liberty, and pursuit of happiness.

NOTES

1. Clarence Page, *Showing My Color: Impolite Essays on Race and Identity* (New York: Perennial, 1996), 20.

2. George F. Will, "Homespun Sport," the *Washington Post* (19 December 1991), first published in the *International Herald Tribune* (November 1991).

3. Will, "Homespun Sport."

4. Will, "Homespun Sport."

5. Will, "Homespun Sport."

6. W.E.B. Du Bois, "The Souls of Black Folk–Of Our Spiritual Strivings," *Writings* (New York: Literary Classics of the United States, 1986), 364–65.

7. Georg Simmel, *Simmel on Culture: Selected Writings*, ed. David Frisby and Mike Featherstone (London: Sage Publications, 1997), 58.

8. Will, "Homespun Sport."

9. See Shane White and Graham White, *African American Expressive Culture from Its Beginnings to the Zoot Suit* (New York: Cornell University Press, 1998), alongside various pieces of commentary and reviews by *Publishers Weekly Review*, *Library Journal*, and *Kirkus Reviews*.

10. Robert Rosen, *A Short History of Charleston* (Charleston: Peninsula Press, 1982), 24.

11. James Draper, "From Slave Cabins to 'Shotguns': Perceptions on Africanisms in American Architecture," *Historia* 10 (Eastern Illinois University, 2001), 82.

12. John Michael Vlach, *The Afro-American Tradition in Decorative Arts* (Athens, GA: University of Georgia Press, 1990), 123.

13. bell hooks, "Architecture and Black Life: Talking Space with Laverne Wells-Bowie," *Art on My Mind: Spatial Politics* (New York: The New Press, 1995), 152–62.

14. hooks, *Art on my Mind,* 147.

15. Mitchell C. Brown, *Index of African American Inventors: Historical*, University of California Irvine, online (accessed March 14, 2015), https://webfiles.uci.edu/mcbrown/display/inventor_list.html.

Liberation is a spatial practice. As a turn on Michel Foucault's axiom that "liberty is a practice," this statement points to how liberation is an action necessitated by the restrictive or oppressive forces of political institutions, infrastructures, and—crucially—their resultant spaces. Foucault's views on the major problems of space derive from an interview with Paul Rabinow titled "Space, Knowledge, and Power," originally published in the architectural journal *Skyline* in March of 1982. Following the industrial revolution, Foucault explains, the problem of space was not just the issue of controlling a territory and governing people within it, but now concerned the spatial relationships between the exercise of power and territory brought on by societal transformations as well as social phenomena resulting from new technologies and new economic processes. Furthermore, in response to the question of whether any particular architectural projects of the past or present act as forces of liberation or resistance, Foucault answers:

> I do not think that it is possible to say that one thing is of the order of "liberation" and another is of the order of "oppression." There are a certain number of things that one can say... but one should still take into account—and this is not generally acknowledged—that, aside from torture and execution, which preclude any resistance, no matter how terrifying a given system may be there always remain the possibilities of resistance, disobedience, and oppositional groupings.[1]

In the face of systemic oppression, Foucault argues, liberatory practices, spatial and otherwise, remain possible.

For African slaves in the American colonies in the eighteenth century, the possibilities of resistance and liberation were, ironically, often to be found in the religious theology of white dominated society; this embrace of an evangelist theology resulted in their own liberative space-making as they constructed spaces for religious worship and refuge. Carter G. Woodson's *A History of the African American Church* (originally published as *The History of the Negro Church* in 1920) chronicles the proselytizing of Negroes as early as 1695 by a white missionary named Rev. Samuel Thomas of Goose Creek Parish in the colony of South Carolina. As the indoctrination and conversion of African slaves spread throughout the American colonies, blacks were allowed to worship in the same space as whites—not as a matter of religious equality, but rather due to a sense of religious paternalism. According to Woodson, Rev. Jonathan Boucher of the Anglican Church boldly stated,

> It certainly is not a necessary circumstance essential to the
> condition of the slave that he be not indoctrinated; yet this
> is the general and almost universal lot of the slaves...You may
> unfetter them from the chains of ignorance, you may emanci-
> pate them from the bondage of sin, the worst slavery to which
> they could be subjected; and thus setting at liberty those that
> are bruised though they still continue to be your slaves, they
> shall be delivered from the bondage of corruption into the glo-
> rious liberty of the children of God.[2]

As the success of indoctrination took hold, a few pioneering Negro preachers emerged, particularly in South Carolina and Georgia. One of these was Andrew Bryan, who was born a slave in 1737 in Goose Creek and was permitted to erect a wood-framed church for his own congregation at Yamacraw (now called Daufuskie Island, South Carolina). However, the congregation was soon dispossessed of the church and forced to hold secret meetings in a nearby swamp in order to evade persecution by the slave master. This, then, is perhaps one of the earliest examples of the subversive space-making of African slaves.

In the 1830s, when all black churches were outlawed following the planning of slave insurrections (led by Gabriel Prosser in Richmond in 1800, Denmark Vesey in Charleston in 1821, and Nat Turner in Southampton County in 1831), the black church went underground and would again have to carve out space in what were called "bush arbors" or "bush harbors", which also denoted a place of security or refuge. These were simple, one room structures, often constructed in the forest out of "brush" or bush tied together with rope or vines in the form of an arbor, underneath which Negro preachers creatively appropriated biblical stories and the religious theology of their slave masters to preach liberation to their fellow slaves. The Works Progress Administration in 1936 documented an account of the bush arbor from Mrs. Amanda Johnson, a former slave born in Glascock, Georgia:

> On the plantation they didn't have no regular church for the
> slaves and so when the weather was good the slaves went to

the woods and had church in a bush arbor. They made a bush
arbor by taking some posts and putting them in the ground
and then covering the top with bushes. Later on they had a
shelter covered with boards. The preaching was done by
an old man they called Caesar—he was too old to do anything
else so preaching was the biggest thing he done.[3]

Recalling the trope of the Abbé Laugier's "primitive hut"—one of the
foundational myths of the Western classical tradition in architecture—these
structures, figuratively and literally carved out of the natural landscape,
were physical and cultural spaces where blacks not only assembled for
worship but also for the purposes of social justice, political action, and
identity formation, set apart and in secret from the patriarchal structures of
slavery, white oppression, and everyday white-dominated society. Hence,
the early black church exploited the condition of "otherness" and constructed an "other" space as well as the foundation for an "other" theology
that would speak to ontological questions related their experience, subjectivity, and identity.

     The role of the black church as a space of liberation later translated
into the liberative promises of social and political justice of the Civil Rights
Movement and in particular Black Liberation Theology, which posits that liberation is the fundamental content of theology. Defined by James H. Cone
in *A Black Theology of Liberation*, black theology emerges out of the need
of blacks to liberate themselves from white oppressors. It is a theology of
liberation which springs from an identification with the oppression of blacks
in America and seeks to interpret religious teachings and biblical history in
light of the black condition.[4] Often rejected as racism when it was first published, Cone sets out in *A Black Theology of Liberation* to create a space
within the dominant theological discourse to address the social, economic,
and political subjugation of black Americans and to take white theology to
task for its failure to recognize the relationships between the black struggle for justice and theological discourse. Cone constructs this space based
upon the spatial praxes of black power extending from insurrectionists like
Prosser, Turner, and Vesey as well as those slaves worshiping in the bush
to defiantly declare, "*I am black because God is black!*" [5] However, black
liberation theology is not static but rather an active practice (as when Cone
speaks of "doing" theology), one which continually recontextualizes theology in relation to the ongoing issues of black liberation. As such, while not

denying deism, Cone states that black theology resembles existentialism in terms of its conviction that existence precedes essence, and that the human subject must be the beginning point of any phenomenological analysis of human existence. Furthermore, the consequences of black liberation theology are inherently spatial and indeed architectural, as it is not only concerned with ontological and existential space but also with the everyday spaces of black life, including community and cultural identity, and social concerns such as poverty, justice, and housing.

Theories of space, subjectivity, and identity—cultural or otherwise—were never the primary concern of the progressive avant-garde of the modern architectural movement. In "The Rise and Fall of the Avant-Garde," Kenneth Frampton recalls that the radical avant-garde emerged as a critique of the *ancien régime* and was invested with full force in the process of modernization in the aftermath of World War I. In the 1920s, this resulted in the positive cultural formations of Purism, Neoplasticism, and Constructivism. In Frampton's account, "the triumphs of science, medicine, and industry seemed to confirm the liberative promise of the modern project," while any questions regarding architecture and the liberative promise of space that pertained to race or cultural subjugation were entirely non-existent.[6]

For Mies van der Rohe and Le Corbusier, two leaders of the radical avant-garde, architecture was an instrument for cultural transformation, the reconstruction and formation of a new society, liberation from nineteenth century bourgeois culture, and the renewed spirit of modernization. While architecture was viewed as being at the service of a generalized European cultural transformation, space was viewed as subservient to the two primary constituents of architecture—namely building and concept. Writing in the first two issues of G in 1923, Mies van der Rohe's polemic makes clear that the "liberation" of modern architecture derives from formalist dogmas:

> We reject { all esthetic speculation,
>   all doctrine,
>   and all formalism.

> Architecture is the will of an epoch translated into space;
> living, changing, new.

> Not yesterday, not tomorrow, only today can be given form.
> Only this kind of building will be creative.
>
> Create form out of the nature of our tasks with the methods of
> our time.
>
> This is our task.
>
> −From G, no. 1
>
> Essentially our task is to free the practice of building from the
> control of esthetic speculators and restore it to what it should
> exclusively be: building.[7]
>
> −From G, no. 2

Accordingly, for Mies van der Rohe architecture was the materialization of the conscious and deliberate transformation of society expressed through the process of the physical construction of the state as manifested in building. Hence, the liberative promise of the modern project was a generalized, free (namely, patriarchal) collective production.

For Le Corbusier, on the other hand, architecture was the intellectual pursuit of the mind and the formulation of an idea translated into a visual experience. *Towards a New Architecture*, Le Corbusier's great manifesto regarding the new epoch of modernization in the first half of the twentieth century, describes how technology, industrial design, and production lead to a new general state of mind. Le Corbusier praises the aesthetics of engineers and excoriates architects for being bound to customs and traditions that stifle the mind. Architecture, defined by contour and profile, is a pure construction of the mind. Le Corbusier states that architecture

> …brings into play the highest faculties by its very abstraction.
> Architectural abstraction has this about it which is magnifi-
> cently peculiar to itself, that while it is rooted in hard fact, it
> spiritualizes it. The naked fact is a medium for an idea only by
> reason of the "order" that is applied to it.
>
> The plan is the generator.
> The eye of the spectator finds itself looking at a site
> composed of streets and houses. It receives the impact of the
> masses which rise up around it. If these masses are of a

formal kind and have not been spoilt by unseemly variations,
if the disposition of their grouping expresses a clean rhythm
and not an incoherent agglomeration, if the relationship
of mass to space is in just proportion, the eye transmits to
the brain coordinated sensations and the mind derives from
these satisfactions of a high order: this is architecture.[8]

Taken together, the liberative promises of the modern architectural project are tied to the technological and abstract intellectual production of a European patriarchy.

In *Architecture as Space: How to Look at Architecture*—first published in Italian in 1948 and published in English in 1957—the Italian architectural historian and critic Bruno Zevi argues that space is the specific property that distinguishes architecture from other forms of art or cultural production. Zevi states that architecture cannot be completely represented in any form, and that it is more than the sum of its two-dimensional representations in the plan or cross-sections of a building, or even in three-dimensional modeling. Architecture, according to Zevi, can only be grasped and felt through direct experience. "To grasp space, to know how to see it, is the key to the understanding of building," Zevi writes. "Until we have learned not only to understand space theoretically, but also to apply this understanding as a central factor in the criticism of architecture, our history, and thus our enjoyment, of architecture will remain haphazard."[9] Furthermore, in his essay "Space—Protagonist of Architecture," Zevi's personification of space implies that subjectivity is tied to spatial experience. The subject is not merely a viewing subject but one capable of identifying with space and grasping meaning. Zevi rejects the functionalism of Le Corbusier and the avant-garde and in contrast constructs a humanist argument for space that is associated with the desire for individual liberation and freedom: "We shall acquire a feeling for space, a love of space, and a need for freedom in space. For space, though it cannot in itself determine our judgment of lyrical values, expresses all the factors of architecture—the sentimental, moral, social and intellectual—and thus represents the precise analytical moment of architecture that is material for its history."[10]

Although for Le Corbusier intellectual production is related to the individual in the personification of the architect or viewer, the question of the individual as an ontological subject conscious of his or her cultural condition is unconsidered. Le Corbusier's subject only *perceives* space and does not experience space or participate in spatial relationships. Furthermore, primacy is given to the architect as author and conceptualizer of the spatial composition from whom all meaning is generated. The lack of consideration to the viewing subject's agency may be due to the fact that science, technology, and reason (three tenets of the new modernization) presuppose a kind of objectivity; their goals are to establish "truths" that are epistemologically objective.

Reflecting upon the early phase of his career as an apprentice in the office of Peter Behrens, Mies van der Rohe states in the March 1961 issue of *Architectural Design* that architecture is a question of such truths. (However, what are the truths for subjugated identities and the practice of spatial freedom or liberation?)

> It then became clear to me that it was not the task of architecture to invent form. I tried to understand what that task was. I asked Peter Behrens, but he could not give me an answer. He did not ask that question. The others said, "What we build is architecture," but we weren't satisfied with this answer. Maybe they didn't understand the question. We tried to find out. We searched in the quarries of ancient and medieval philosophy. Since we know that it was a question of the truth, we tried to find out what the truth really was. We were very delighted to find a definition of truth by St. Thomas Aquinas: "Adequatio intellectus et rei" or as a modern philosopher expresses it in the language of today: "Truth is the significance of fact." I never forgot this. It was very helpful, and has been a guiding light. To find out what architecture really is took me fifty years—half a century.[11]

Subsequent to Mies' search for the truths of architecture, Team X, the rebellious progeny of the radical avant-garde from whom the movements of New Brutalism and Structuralism emerged, put forth an architecture based upon the ideas of community identity and urban sociology in the 1960s. While their work did approach a sense of fine-grained context with the promise of a more specific social and cultural role for modernist architecture, their proposals ironically remained patriarchal and even paternalistic given the Oedipal relationship between themselves and their predecessors. Yet the questions of subjectivity and cultural awareness continued to remain unexplored and unanswered.

It may be argued that questions of space, subjectivity, and cultural identity formation are constructions of the second half of the twentieth century, rooted in identity theory and later taken up by Jacques Lacan in his writings on experience and subjectivity—although for Lacan, experience is determinative of *language* rather than subject/object relations. Henri Lefebvre refutes Lacan's thesis that defines space as a pre-existing, neutral, and objective condition that can be simply read as the space of speech and writing and instead argues that space is a social product and the result of spatial praxes within a given context. In *The Production of Space* (originally published in 1974), Lefebvre cites Le Corbusier's avant-gardist position as working towards a "technicist, scientific, and intellectualized representation of space" rather than the making of representational space, which Lefebvre defines as the space of inhabitants and users as well as artists and philosophers who desire more than to describe space.[12] Lefebvre states:

> In reality, social space 'incorporates' social actions, the actions of subjects both individual and collective who are born and who die, who suffer and who act. From the point of view of these subjects, the behavior of their space is at once vital and mortal: within it they develop, give expression to themselves, and encounter prohibitions; then they perish, and that same space contains their graves. From the point of view of knowing (*connaissance*), social space works (along with its concept) as a tool for the analysis of society.[13]

It would not be until the late avant-garde of the 1970s and 1980s that these questions of subjectivity and representational space would inform art and architectural criticism through the heterogeneous practices of post-structuralism, giving way to the exploration of a host of discursive spaces (including race, gender, class, and cultural subjugation) in reaction to the dominant European patriarchal narratives of modernism and the early avant-garde.

While cultural subjugation in terms of identity politics or race were not considered during the sixteenth and seventeenth centuries, issues of space and subjectivity were at work during the late Italian Renaissance and Baroque periods of art and architectural history, and many of the representations of mass oppression as well as individual liberation through a divine subject/object relationship were of biblical stories that African slaves in the American colonies creatively identified with and appropriated in their struggle for freedom. Although African slaves were not aware of these particular works of art, Renaissance drawings and religious paintings as well as the interiors of Italian Renaissance and Baroque churches made specific use of linear perspective techniques in order to construct direct spatial relationships between the viewer (or subject) and theological doctrines; these relationships point to the liberative potentials of theological space. In particular, during the Counter-Reformation of the sixteenth and seventeenth centuries, the Catholic Church sought to restore its predominance and centrality through architecture, painting, and sculpture that reaffirmed the Church's omniscience and Catholic theology. Borne from the deliberations of the Council of Trent in December 1563, Baroque painting and sculpture focused on the incontrovertible dogma of the Church with the primary figures slightly elevated and at the focal point of the composition in order to reinforce the hierarchy of church doctrine relative to the viewer. Furthermore, the Church commissioned art works that were intended to be direct, compelling, and as understandable to the ordinary viewer as possible. Although the works were intended to contain a new realism, the representation of biblical stories still maintained an authoritative position, with a viewer's subjectivity subservient to the omniscience of the Church. This is evident in the work of the three Carraccis—brothers Agostino and Annibale and cousin Ludovico. In particular, the 1591 painting by Ludovico Carracci entitled *The Holy Family with St. Francis* maintains the Renaissance hierarchy of the painting's central figures: the Virgin and Child in an elevated position on a high throne, St. Francis kneeling at the left, and St. Joseph seated below at the right and gazing up at the Holy Family. [1] However, these spatial relationships are intended to draw the viewer into space of the painting. Ludovico's figures are deeply engrossed; subtle gestures and glances humanize the central figures and create an empathetic relationship between the subjects in the painting and the viewer. Additionally, the figures are represented with mass and weight that renders their presence, and the close viewpoint breaks down the barrier between the space of the painting and space of the viewing subject. Yet Ludovico's patterns of light and dark, falling principally upon the Virgin and

Child, ensure a sense of mystery and suggest that, despite their presence and apparent nearness, they remain in a world beyond that of the viewer. Rudolf Wittkower, in *Art and Architecture in Italy: 1600–1750*, states that "Ludovico's whole trend in these years is towards the colossal, the passionate, dramatic, and heroic, towards rich movement and surprising and capricious light effects…"[14]

While Ludovico Carracci's painting moves away from classicism and the mannerist style of the late Renaissance, it is Michelangelo Merisi da Caravaggio's paintings after 1606 (when he fled Rome after being charged with manslaughter) that radically challenge the spatial compositions of the late Renaissance as well as the spatial order of Counter-Reformation religious dogma and theology. In his 1609 *Raising of Lazarus*, Caravaggio liberates the space of the painting by breaking the frame of the canvas to establish a mise-en-scène that captures the dynamic movement of space in a cinematic instant. [2] The primary figures in the scene move across the bottom of the canvas while carrying Lazarus' limp body, at a diagonal with outstretched arms and legs, implying multiple spatial vectors that refer to the dark, unknown spaces in the painting. Secondly, the figure of Christ is located not at the center but at the left edge of the painting, pointing toward Lazarus. The figures carrying Lazarus appear to be looking past the figure of Christ towards a space outside the frame of the canvas. Additionally, while the scene appears to be compressed at the picture frame of the viewer's perspective, the vast areas of darkness beyond and above the figures suggest the "unknown" and the questioning of Counter-Reformation theology that intended to re-establish itself as predominant and omniscient. The weight of the areas of darkness in the painting appear to be equal to the dynamic use of light that illuminates Lazarus, the faces of the on-lookers, and the multiple spatial vectors, all while casting the face of Christ in shadow.[15] The spatial composition of the painting points to the special meaning the story of Lazarus holds in the black church as one of hope and liberation (even from death) despite darkness, pain, and suffering. As the dynamic movement in the painting appears to extend beyond the frame and the gazes of the figures look towards an unknown space, the oral tradition of this story from African slaves through to present day black theology recenters subjectivity within the direct spatial and cultural experience of everyday life.

The recentering of subjectivity found in Caravaggio's post-Rome paintings eventually makes its way into the architectural space of the church itself, notably in the design of San Carlo Alle Quattro Fontane (1634–41) and St. Ivo della Sapienza (1642–50) by the architect Francesco Borromini. Borromini not only challenges late Renaissance spatial composition and the subject/object relationship between the viewing subject and the Church, but also reconceptualizes the representation of theology by abandoning the anthropomorphism that had defined spatial composition until then. This created architecture that was not representative of the body but rather that engaged the body in a spatial experience, set in perpetual motion and grounded in sensuality. In describing Borromini's contemporaries' assessment of his work and his introduction of "a new and disturbing approach to old problems," Wittkower states, "When Bernini talked in Paris about Borromini, all agreed, according to the Sieur de Chantelou, that his architecture was extravagant and in striking contrast to normal procedure; whereas the design of a building, it was argued, usually depended on the proportions of the human body, Borromini had broken with this tradition and erected fantastic ('chimerical') structures."[16] The noted Borromini scholar Sir Anthony Blunt declares more forcefully:

> He attains his effects by purely architectural means, and in devising these he showed the utmost inventiveness. His spaces flow into one another; walls are curved or articulated in depth by columns and niches; he uses novel forms of arches, sometimes twisting them in three dimensions, and he invents fantastic forms for his domes, belfries and lanterns. The result is an architecture in which the essentially Baroque feature of movement is given its most brilliant expression, undisturbed by the distractions of color, richness of materials or drama. One looks at Bernini's buildings with the eyes; one feels Borromini's with the whole body.[17]

As such, Borromini prioritizes the ontological questions of subjectivity, human experience, and understanding over questions of deism, which are taken as matter of fact, thereby creating liberative spatial experiences.

While there is little written evidence from Borromini himself regarding his theories about architecture, the introduction to the *Opus Architectonicum*, with engravings of Borromini's Oratory of S. Filippo Neri, provides some insight. According to Blunt, the text was prepared by Virgilio Spada, the Prior of the Oratory when Borromini worked on the design, but it is written in the first person, suggesting that it is actually the architect's own statement. Taken together with other contemporaneous writings on Borromini's work, it becomes clear that he was indeed a conscious innovator. Blunt argues that in the *Opus Architectonicum*, "the architect says that his intention is to produce 'new things' and not 'conventional designs' but justifies his intention by referring to Michelangelo, who did likewise, and quoting his remark that 'one who follows others never gets ahead of them.'" [18] Furthermore, Borromini reveals the origins of his unsettling designs in the geometric construction of lines and points in drawings prepared by his own hands. The drawings for both San Carlo and St. Ivo reveal a series of geometrical operations using triangles, circles, and arcs that point out Borromini's interest in the language of mathematics as it is associated with science, philosophy, and theology, and results in his subversive space-making and reconceptualization of subjectivity.

Widely considered among art historians are the relationships between Borromini's work and the writings of Galileo, who was suspected of heresy by the Inquisition in 1611 and later forced to live under house arrest for his Copernican views regarding the solar system. Art historian Joseph Connors, in "S. Ivo Alla Sapienza: The First Three Minutes," surmises that the conduit for the relationship between Borromini and Galileo was Fra Benedetto Castelli, who had given Borromini drawings of San Vitale in Ravenna, but more importantly, had been Galileo's student in Padua in 1604 and became lifelong friends with him. Castelli, who was also a professor of mathematics at the Sapienza when Borromini designed St. Ivo, exchanged hundreds of letters with Galileo which shed light on the fact that the study of geometry had become quite fashionable in the Barberini court of Pope Urban VIII—who also happened to be Borromini's patron. Furthermore, Connors points out that Castelli's successor at the Sapienza in 1643 was another former pupil of Galileo named Gaspare Berti, "who also knew Borromini and once even made a model for the architect." [19] Finally, art historian John Hatch speculates on the relationship between Borromini's designs and the writings of Johannes Kepler. Hatch postulates, "It is specifically in the writings of Johannes Kepler that one finds the most consistent explanation for Borromini's use of geometry in architecture, as well as a source for the unusual cosmological Trinitarian references found at the churches of S. Carlo alle Quattro Fontane and S. Ivo della Sapienza." [20]

Kepler, the German astronomer and mathematician who discovered three major laws of planetary motion including the discovery of the first law in 1605 (that the planets move in elliptical orbits around the Sun), sought the intersection of astronomy, mathematics, and theology in his work. In his *Mysterium Cosmographicum* of 1596, he posited a model of the universe that not only explained the spacing of the six Copernican planets (at that time still thought to be set in circular orbits), demonstrated by inscribing each orbit within a nested regular polyhedron, but also argued that the entire system inscribed within a sphere symbolized the Christian Trinity. [3] In 1621 he revised the *Mysterium Cosmographicum* in light of his discoveries regarding planetary motion. Yet the significance of this early work is Kepler's use of geometry to spatialize the matrix of science, mathematics, and theology. In San Carlo alle Quattro Fontane, Borromini's complex use of geometry can be read as putting Kepler's matrix into continuous and dynamic motion, orbiting around the interior volume of the church with a multiplicity of viewpoints rather than a single honorific position of a theological subject/object relationship. The planar geometry of the church consists of two tangential circles whose center points locate the foci of the ellipse which is generally inscribed in the overall plan and which determines the base of the dome of the church. Each circle is in turn inscribed within an equilateral triangle such that the triangles share a common base. However, a more detailed analysis reveals that the triangles are inscribed within a pair of overlapping circles that establish the general depth and thickness of the plan. Hence, it is this pair of circles that sets the space in an elliptical orbit and spatializes Kepler's first law of planetary motion. [4] Furthermore, Borromini uses a system of secondary arcs to deform the inside surface of the ellipse, thereby making the orbit undulate and intensifying the sense of motion and the direct relationship between the subject and the spatial experience of the church. Horizontal bands along the surface of the interior track movement around the space, and overlapping columns provide a triple metered rhythm with short and long pauses. [5] Decorative motifs in the coffering of the dome diminish in size as the decorations reach the base of the lantern. This accentuates the verticality of the space and suggests a feeling of reaching the cosmos in an apparent swirling motion, resulting from the play of day-lighting emanating from windows at the base of the dome and across the coffering of the hemispherical space. At the exterior of the church, the use of arcs and geometric manipulations undulate the façade, causing a disruption along the urban street wall and a corporeal and cosmic disturbance at the intersection of Via del Quirinale and Via delle Quattro Fontane.

While the interior of St. Ivo della Sapienza appears more restrained than San Carlo, the radicality of the interior spatial experience is no less considered. Connors cites as a source for the design a sketch made by Carlo Maderno or Van Zantern in 1612 or 1613 resembling a Gothic ornamentation of triangles-with-apses and truncated corners.[21] Maderno was Borromini's mentor and master when he arrived in Rome from Milan in 1619. Connors furthermore cites a sketch by Baldassarre Peruzzi as being the closet precedent for St. Ivo: "The triangle in Peruzzi's drawing provided the basic armature; wall thicknesses were added almost as an afterthought. Two of the angles are cut off by niches with flat faces, while the third angle becomes an entrance with a columnar porch and vestibule like a mini-Pantheon."[22] Again, a closer inspection of the plan reveals a relationship to Kepler's model of the universe as a nested polyhedron inscribed within a sphere.

The plan geometry, which is imperceptible to the viewing subject at the interior of the church, consists of two overlapping equilateral triangles centered upon the outline of a circle. [6] Yet the overlapping triangles can also be circumscribed by a circle tangential to and in opposition to the curved façade of the church's courtyard elevation. This overall geometry is enclosed within the half sphere of the dome. A series of columns define the intersecting points of the triangles and circles and extend the plan geometry to the base of the dome. The lines of force defined by the columns paradoxically emphasize a visually upward movement rather than a downward movement and are translated into the pilasters of the dome. However, a ring of windows in the drum of the lantern creates a halo of light that separates the cupola from the dome and seemingly projects the space into a condition of boundlessness. [7] At the exterior, the upward energy of the interior is translated into a spiral atop the lantern that ignites a flaming laurel crown beneath a floating sphere.

While it cannot be claimed that Borromini engaged in a direct translation of Kepler's theories, Borromini did radicalize architecture through the reconceptualization of space. He also made the experience of space, and by extension subjectivity, the existential question for the discipline and the making of architecture. Borromini united the conception of space with the perception of space to yield "experienced space." In a foreshadow to Lefebvre, Borromini transformed the scientific and theological *representations of space* into *representational spaces* such that the visceral conditions of San Carlo alle Quattro Fontane and St. Ivo della Sapienza liberate the subject from theological dogma and produce new subjectivities related to bodily lived experience. In fact, Borromini may be considered the first "space architect", a moniker bestowed upon the architect R.M. Schindler by Esther McCoy, noted architectural historian and one-time draftsman in Schindler's office, in a 1945 article in the left-wing, East Coast art journal *Direction.* In the article, McCoy describes Schindler's design process, use of geometry, and his concern for the design of spatial experience over the implementation of formalist dogmas, exemplified in his design for a black Baptist congregation in South Los Angeles in 1944.

In 1933, following the Great Depression and at the beginning of the Second Great Migration—in which many African Americans moved from the South to the western states, Los Angeles, and southern California—a group of 240 congregants organized the Bethlehem Baptist Church in South Los Angeles. At the turn of the century during the original Great Migration, blacks had quietly migrated to Los Angeles from states like Texas, Louisiana, and Georgia in order to escape the racial oppression and subjugation of the South. Given their relatively small population, blacks lived with a sense of free will and were rooted in a much more complex and diverse sense of black identity. As this population increased during the Second Great Migration, with blacks seeking economic opportunities as well as freedom, so did the sense of community. Many newly arriving blacks from the South also brought their theological beliefs, and the Baptist denomination soon significantly outnumbered others in Los Angeles. The historical strength of Baptist theology among blacks can be traced to the fact that the Baptist Church in the South opposed slavery during the eighteenth century. Carter G. Woodson writes, "The Baptists reached their most advanced position as an anti-slavery body in 1789 when they took action to the effect 'that slavery is a violent depredation of the rights of nature and inconsistent with a republican government, and therefore, recommend it to our brethren, to make use of their local missions to extirpate this horrid evil from the land.'" [23]

The Bethlehem Baptist congregation purchased an existing church building, built in 1918, for two thousand dollars, but a fire destroyed the building in 1943 and the church then sought an architect to design a new building on property acquired from a German Methodist congregation at 49th Street and Compton Avenue. The first design for the church was prepared by James Homer Garrott, a licensed black architect who had graduated from Los Angeles Polytechnic High School in 1917, earned his architectural license in 1928 and established his own practice, and later studied architecture at the University of South California in the early 1930s. Garrott's design was a traditional large sanctuary with a gabled façade, three arched windows, and an attached bell tower through which members entered the church. The church was sited at the corner of the property with a strip of grass surrounding the building. Steve Wallet—whose essay "From South Los Angeles to West Hollywood: James Garrott, Rudolph Schindler, and the Bethlehem Baptist Church" is one of the few to address this little-known building—describes Garrott's design as a rectangular worship space with a raised pulpit and choir loft opposite the entry to the church at Compton Avenue.[24]

It is clear from the description that the design was based upon a typ-ical and un-extraordinary church plan. The latest drawings prepared by Garrott are dated May 22, 1944 and signed by the Reverend C.J. Hall, the young pastor of the church who had only been elected to that position in March of 1944. Rev. Hall arrived in Los Angeles from Atlanta where he had studied at the Gammon Theological Seminary and at Morehouse College during the presidency of Dr. Benjamin E. Mays, the great educator, so-ciologist, social activist, and mentor to Martin Luther King, Jr. However, by August 31, 1944, R. M. Schindler (a European émigré who was not yet fa-mous at the time) had been hired by the church to develop an entirely new design. This could have been due in part to the church's limited construc-tion budget of $20,000, or, as Esther McCoy recorded in her unpublished essay, "Bethlehem Baptist Church Story", the hiring of Schindler could have had more ambitious causes: "…But says the present pastor, the Rev. C.C. Brooks, 'Some of the congregation had the idea that the church should reach toward the future as well as the past.'"[25]

Schindler took a radically different approach from his predecessor, locating the church at the southeast corner of the site away from the inter-section of cross streets to establish a diagonal site condition. Additionally, and perhaps more importantly, Schindler bifurcated the traditional subject/object (Baptist "call and response") relationship between preacher and congregants and split the relationship open along the diagonal, resulting in two perpendicular (and intersecting axes). [8] The split yields an abstraction and displacement of the traditional cruciform plan iconography and instead places an emphasis on the individual subject's relationship to the interior spatial experience through the focused sight lines of the resulting bisection. Additionally, this operation produces an opening from the exterior patio to the interior, above which sits a skylight topped with intersecting planes that form a cruciform tower. [9, 10] Schindler described the cruciform tower as a departure from the two-dimensional cross, which is a symbol of pain and suffering; instead, the arms of the cruciform tower are outstretched and embracing. Conversely, the split produces a spatial extension from the interior towards the exterior and reach of the church from the site to the community. Schindler stated,

> In the usual church the congregation arrives, finds pews, and sits until service is over. Then they stand on the public side walk in front of the church to chat. There is no freedom of movement. People are incidental to the church. But in the Bethlehem Baptist people are needed to complete the picture. When the congregation begins to gather on a Sunday morning, they have a place to stand and talk. There they get the feel of the community. Only modern architecture takes into account this social aspect of a church.[26]

Additionally, Schindler's notes regarding the design point out that he was keenly aware of the importance of social life, the sense of refuge in the black church, and that despite the promises of the Southern California dream there existed certain places where blacks were not welcomed. Restrictive covenants were frequently used by real estate developers and planning boards to keep blacks out or run the risk of violent real estate conflicts. A line in his notes simply states: "Social aspect of church, especially Negro, who need security."[27] Hence, Schindler creates a spatial relay between interior subjectivities and the communal black identity represented by the patio space, as well as the future city growing up around the church. The exterior of the church, constructed of wood and stucco and rendered as austere white planes, is a result of the multiple horizontal vectors that overlap and extend the theological space into a constructivist, spatial composition reaching towards an infinite future. [11] In "Schindler, Space

Architect," Esther McCoy, who worked on the Bethlehem Baptist Church design while in Schindler's office, writes:

> In the Bethlehem Baptist Church, a Negro church in the
> east part of Lost Angeles, he discarded all the clichés of ec-
> clesiastical usage without on the other hand indulging in
> extraneous brilliant techniques. He simply made a gracious
> statement in wood and glass. He pulled down the drafting ma-
> chine, clicked it at 45 degrees, and moved the scales rapidly
> along the drawing. He clicked it again, then cruised between
> 45 degrees and 49 degrees for a while… He designs and
> builds in terms of space forms rather than mass forms. His
> houses are wrapped around space. You can quickly see in his
> space forms how he has created a new definition for space;
> a Schindler house is in movement; it is in becoming.[28]

Tellingly, McCoy's account is quite similar to Sir Anthony Blunt's statement regarding the spatial experiences of Borromini's architecture. Schindler, like Borromini, transforms representations of space into representational spaces that collapse concept and perception into experience. [12]

Furthermore, at the Bethlehem Baptist Church, Schindler transforms the hegemony of theological space that had been handed down from white missionaries to slaves in the eighteenth century into a liberative space that switches between individual subjectivity and community identity, and antic-ipates the relationship between liberation and what would be called "black theology" nearly thirty years later. Finally, Schindler, a contemporary of the European radical avant-garde architects led by Le Corbusier and Mies van der Rohe, achieves what the early modern architectural movement failed to consider—namely, the promise of space to practice liberation and cultural identity. In his 1912 manifesto, "Modern Architecture: A Program", written in Vienna before he immigrated to the United States, Schindler declared:

> The architectural design concerns itself with "Space" as its
> raw material and with the articulated room as its product.
> …
> The architect has finally discovered the medium of his art:
> S P A C E.
> A new architectural problem has been born.[29]

NOTES

1. Michel Foucault, "Space, Knowledge, and Power," interview with Paul Rabinow in *The Foucault Reader* (New York: Pantheon Books, 1984), 245.

2. Carter G. Woodson, *A History of the African American Church* (Washington, DC: Associated Publishers, 1920; reprinted New York: Diasporic Africa Press, Inc.), 4–13.

3. Federal Writers Project, *Georgia Slave Narratives: A Folk History of Slavery in the United States from Interviews with Former Slaves* (Native American Book Publishers, 1938), 292.

4. James H. Cone, *A Theology of Black Liberation* (New York: J.B. Lippincott Company, 1970; reprinted Maryknoll, NY: Orbis Press, 1986), 5.

5. Cone, *A Theology of Black Liberation*, 80.

6. Kenneth Frampton, "The Rise and Fall of the Avant-Garde," from "Towards a Critical Regionalism: Six Points for an Architecture of Resistance," in *The Anti-Aesthetic: Essays on Postmodern Culture* (New York: Bay Press, 1995), 18.

7. Mies van der Rohe, "1922: Two Glass Skyscrapers," republished in Philip Johnson's *Mies van der Rohe* (New York: Museum of Modern Art, 1947), 182.

8. Le Corbusier, *Towards a New Architecture* (London: J. Rodker, 1931; reprinted New York: Dover Publications, Inc., 1986), 47.

9. Bruno Zevi, *Architecture as Space: How to Look at Architecture* (New York: Horizon Press, 1957), 23.

10. Zevi, *Architecture as Space,* 242.

11. Peter Carter, "Mies van der Rohe: An Appreciation on the Occasion of his 75th Birthday," *Architectural Design,* v. 31, no. 3 (March 1961), 97.

12. Henri Lefebvre, *The Production of Space,* trans. Donald Nicholson-Smith (Oxford: Blackwell, 1992), 39–43.

13. Lefebvre, *The Production of Space,* 33–34.

14. Rudolf Wittkower, *Art and Architecture in Italy 1600–1750* (Harmondsworth, Middlesex, England: Penguin Books Ltd., 1986), 62.

15. Wittkower, *Art and Architecture in Italy*, 54. In his examination of the ramifications of Caravaggio's late work, Wittkower states: "The setting of Caravaggio's pictures is usually outside the realm of daily life. His figures occupy a narrow foreground close to the beholder. Their attitudes and movements, their sudden foreshortenings into an undefined void, heighten the beholder's suspense by giving a tense sensation of impenetrable space. But despite, or because of, its irrationality, his light has the power to reveal and to conceal."

16. Wittkower, *Art and Architecture in Italy,* 197.

17. Anthony Blunt, *Borromini* (Cambridge, MA: The Belknap Press of Harvard University Press, 1979), 24.

18. Blunt, *Borromini*, 27.

19. Joseph Connors, "S. Ivo Alla Sapienza: The First Three Minutes," *Journal of the Society of Architectural Historians* 55 (1996), 52.

20. John G. Hatch, "The Science Behind Francesco Borromini's Divine Geometry," *Visual Arts Publications*, Paper 4 (2002), 127.

21. Connors, "S. Ivo Alla Sapienza: The First Three Minutes," 46.

22. Connors, "S. Ivo Alla Sapienza: The First Three Minutes," 47.

23. Woodson, *A History of the African American Church*, 17.

24. Steve Wallet, "From South Los Angeles to West Hollywood: James Garrott, Rudolph Schindler and the Bethlehem Baptist Church" (June 17, 2014), stevewallet.com.

25. Esther McCoy, "Bethlehem Baptist Church Story" (c.1939, undated and unpublished), Esther McCoy papers, 1876–1990, bulk, 1938–1989, Archives of American Art, Series 6: Architect Files, 1912–1990, box 24, folder 10, 1, http://www.aaa.si.edu/collections/container/viewer/-Bethlehem-Baptist-Church-Story--343462.

26. McCoy, "Bethlehem Baptist Church Story," box 24, folder 10, 2.

27. McCoy, "Bethlehem Baptist Church Story," box 24, folder 10.

28. Esther McCoy, "Schindler, Space Architect," in *Piecing Together Los Angeles: An Esther McCoy Reader* (Valencia: East of Borneo, 2012), 72–73.

29. See R.M. Schindler, "Modern Architecture: A Program," in August Sarnitz, *R.M. Schindler, Architect, 1887–1953* (New York: Rizzoli, 1988).

In his *Theory of the Avant-Garde*, Peter Burger sets out a fully elaborated theory of the "institution of art" and critiques the avant-garde's inability to resist that process of institutionalization. Burger states:

> Now that the attack of the historical avant-garde movements
> on art as an institution has failed, and art has not been
> integrated into the praxis of life, art as an institution continues
> to serve as something separate from the praxis of life. But
> the attack did make art recognizable as an institution
> and also revealed its relative inefficacy in bourgeois society
> as its principle.[1]

Furthermore, Burger asserts that attempts by neo-avant-garde movements to attain the protest value of the historical avant-garde are flawed from the outset—the techniques of the avant-gardes have lost their shock value, he argues, and the hope that art could be sublimated into everyday life has proven false. "To formulate more pointedly: the neo-avant-garde institutionalizes the avant-garde as art and thus negates genuinely avant-gardist intentions."[2]

While Burger's argument—including the salient illustration of the degree to which resistance can be co-opted—is not without merit, his analysis misses certain ways in which the art of the neo-avant-gardes still held certain forms of political potency. The genealogy of the work produced by neo-avant-garde artists in the 1970s and 1980s does in fact run from Dada through Duchamp; however, these artists sought to extend the practices of the modernist avant-garde by way of creative analyses, while taking the institutionalization that Burger notes as a site for critique. Artists such as Martha Rosler, Louise Lawler, Sherrie Levine, Jenny Holzer, Barbara Kruger, and even Dan Graham and Richard Prince moved beyond the "transgressive objects" of the historical avant-garde to think instead about strategies, operations, and practices that addressed the seriality of objects and images within commercial capitalism, while also exploring markers of physical presence, material definition, and site (whether physical, social, or linguistic). Additionally, these later artists sought to question art's mode of address and its audience, thus rethinking the function of aesthetic practices within the institutions of modernism.

These new artistic praxes were meant to address ideological discourses outside of institutional frameworks—rather than being subsumed within them—and to probe the spaces of sexual identity, ethnic identity, and so-cial difference.[3] Working within the contemporary milieus of conceptual and performance art—while still making use of certain Dadaist devices—the artist Adrian Piper, for example, introduced questions of racial subjectiv-ity into the vocabulary of conceptual art, demonstrating that racial identity is spatialized and informed by experience. Hence, artists like Piper not only attacked the institutionalization of art (including the historical avant-garde) but also the hegemony of white male subjectivity relative to the produc-tion of the art object, its commodification and exclusion of difference, and the discourse of art itself. Their works are a direct refutation of Burger's contention that "the Neo-avant-garde, which stages for a second time the avant-gardist break with tradition, becomes a manifestation that is void of sense and permits the positing of any meaning whatever."[4] Instead, taken together, the radical artists of the 1970's and 1980's neo-avant-garde ex-posed discursive spaces that problematized the relationships between subject and art object, and critiqued institutional art practices by reworking the historical avant-garde in terms of formal language, cultural-political strategies, and social positioning.

In doing so, they also provided space for radical architecture, whose goal was not form but the politics of space. Their conceptual practices allowed architects such as Bernard Tschumi to replace questions of formal language with questions of relationships and space—concept, experience, and implicit questions of subjectivity. That the strategies and practices of these artists critiqued construction of subjectivity, representation, and identity in terms of spatial relationships and praxes rather than signifiers, symbols, and mimetic images suggests tactics by which architecture might overcome the burdens of representation in the address of racial identity and cultural experience.

During the historical avant-garde, the Berlin Dadaists George Grosz, John Heartfield, and Raoul Hausmann derived techniques from mass media to create works with fragments of photographs, text, and found objects. These were disassociated from their original context, disassembled, recombined, and reconfigured in a way to create new meaning; likewise, Dadaist po-etry depleted words, syllables, and sounds of their traditional semantic functions, forms, and references until they became visually and concretely present. The Dadaists were the most outspoken critics and antagonists of Expressionism, and of bourgeois art, politics, and society.

As Hans Richter wrote in his introduction to *Dada: Kunst und Antikunst* (1965), the Dadaist sought direct engagement, if not confrontation, with the present, as well as the internal contradictions, doubt, chaos, flux, and chance forces of life. Dadaists used photomontage in opposition to the increasing aestheticism and formalism of collage (which Richter dismissed as "pieces of paper and cloth stuck on to a picture, which had already been tried") in order to create, often from totally disparate spatial and material elements, a new unity that was to reveal a visually and conceptually new image of chaos in an age of war and revolution.[5] Richter quotes George Grosz in *Dada: Kunst und Antikunst* recalling that in 1916, when he and John Heartfield

> invented photomontage in my studio at the south end of
> the town at five o'clock one May morning, we had no idea of
> the immense possibilities, or of the thorny but successful
> career, that awaited the new invention. On a piece of card-
> board we pasted a mischmasch of advertisements for
> hernia belts, student song-books and dog food, labels from
> schnapps—and wine—bottles, and photographs from pic-
> ture papers, cut up at will in such a way as to say, in pictures,
> what would have been banned by the censors if we had said
> it in words. In this way we made postcards supposed to have
> been sent home from the Front, or from home to the Front.[6]

Dadaist photomontages employed not only techniques of montage, but also of appropriation, which served to challenge points of view and perspectives. These works upended the idealist, humanist cosmology of Expressionism with contrasts of tone, structure, dimension, technical flexibility, and clear formal dialectics that represented the reality of everyday life through the Dadaist lens. [13] The scale of these Dadaist photomon-tages ranged from the tabletop "mischmasch" described by Grosz to full-scale installations at exhibitions such as the 1920 First International "Dada-Messe," or Dada Fair, in Berlin. This event was the climax of the movement's public activities and was held at a bookshop gallery owned by Dr. Otto Burchardt (who was also known to the group as "Finanz-Dada"). Furthermore, Grosz, Heartfield, and Hausmann realized that the operations they performed on representational images or sounds produced power-ful programmatic interruptions, interferences, and propagandistic effects. Hausmann stated in 1931:

> In the conflict of opinions people often argue that photomon-tage is only possible in two ways: one being the political, the other being the commercial. ... The Dadaists, after having "in-vented" the static, the simultaneous, and the purely phonetic poem, now applied the same principles with consequence to pictorial representation. In the medium of photography they were the first to create from structural elements of often very heterogeneous material or locales a new unity that tore a visu-ally and cognitively new mirror image from the period of chaos in war and revolution; and they knew that their method had an inherent propagandistic power that contemporary life was not courageous enough to absorb and to develop.[7]

This fact became significant to the avant-garde of the 1970s and 1980s as a theory of allegory and montage that describes how if language and image were taken into the service of advertising, that trajectory could be subverted by appropriating the languages of mass media (television, adver-tising, and photography) and subjecting the idea of everyday life to a set of formal, spatial, and linguistic operations. These operations included the splintering of the signifier from the signified, the dismantling of hierarchi-cal ordering systems, and the transformation of larger social structures. For "the procedure of montage," as Benjamin Buchloh puts it, "is one in which all allegorical principles are executed: appropriation and depletion of mean-ing, fragmentation and dialectical juxtaposition of fragments, and separation of signifier and signified."[8]

In New York Dada, these early motives were most apparent in the ready-mades of Duchamp. Buchloh argues that in the case of the ready-mades,

> the willful declaration of the unaltered object as meaningful and the act of its appropriation allegorized creation by brack-eting it with the anonymous mass-produced object. With Duchamp's ready-mades it seems that the traditional sepa-ration of the pictorial or sculptural construct into procedures and materials of construction, a pictorial signifier,

and a signified does not occur—rather all three coalesce in the
allegorical gesture of appropriating the object and of negating
the actual construction of the sign. At the same time, this emphasis on the manufactured signifier and its mute existence
makes apparent the hidden factors determining the work and
the conditions under which it is perceived. Such factors range
from presentational devices and the institutional framework
to the conventions of meaning-assignment within art itself.[9]

Duchamp's investigations into the relationship between subject and art
object—undertaken by changing the status of the everyday object and its
understanding by displacing it into a new context—prefigure the work of
neo-avant-garde artists of the 1970s New York scene.

Martha Rosler's *House Beautiful: Bringing the War Home* series
(1967–72), to take one example, uses photomontage of housekeeping advertisements and mass-media domestic environments together with images
of war culled from *Life* magazine to protest the war in Vietnam. [14, 15]
Rosler explains that the work emanated from "frustration with the images
we saw in television and print media, even with anti-war flyers and posters.
The images we saw were always very far away, in a place we couldn't imag-
ine."[10] Rosler's work reveals the artificiality of this severed relationship
between consumer media and the political and economic realities of war.
The work also contrasts the brutality and androcentrism of war with the
changes happening in the interior domestic environment, which was being
transformed by the Women's Liberation Movement.

In Rosler's photomontages, these relationships are played out in the
domestic spaces of the kitchen, the bedroom, and the living room sofa.
The Vietnam War was the first "television war" to be viewed remotely from
the comfortable confines of domestic space, and Rosler sought to re-
connect the two sides of this human experience. Therefore, in a series of
allegorical investigations, the relationships between signifier and signified
reveal the dissociation between subject and object within the consumer-
valued context of advertising, and subjectivity is repositioned within the political and economic space between the living room and the battlefield.
The *Bringing the War Home* series connects its visual foregrounds with
its infrastructural backgrounds by stitching the two together in a jump-cut
of space and time, a technique that was first theorized in the late 1910s
films and writings of Sergei Eisenstein and developed further by radical

filmmakers of the 1960s and '70s. Laura Cottingham, in a catalog essay that accompanies this photographic series, argues that Rosler's work

> draws on the disjunctive technical style and consumer-
> capitalism critiques of French New Wave director Jean-Luc
> Godard, who Rosler acknowledges as a major influence. In
> fact, Godard's *Ici et Ailleurs* (Here and Elsewhere, 1974),
> produced after Rosler finished this series, explores the
> same contradiction suggested in *Bringing the War Home*:
> French consumerism (here) and the Palestinian struggle
> (elsewhere).[11]

Hence, the jump-cuts in Rosler's work collapse "here" and "there" into a temporal simultaneity that interrupts the unconscious consumption of war and the socio-political everyday of domesticity.

In September 1978, the curator Janelle Reiring invited Louise Lawler, Adrian Piper, Cindy Sherman, and Christopher D'Arcangelo to participate in a group show at Artists Space in New York. These artists' installations shared an interest in exposing power relations and rethinking the institutional obligations of an alternative arts organization, as well as the relationships between the viewer and the work of art. Through techniques of appropriation, withdrawal, direct address, and redirection, the artists reflected these concerns back onto the role of the viewer. In *The Proposal for Artists Space*, Reiring's text that framed the ideas of the show, she described it as

> a group exhibition of artists concerned with how they present
> work. The proposed artists are essentially outsiders look-
> ing at the social, economic, and political aspects of the art
> world. Their work reflects an analysis of the art-world sys-
> tem, and their individual attempts to develop strategies to
> deal with it. At this point in their careers, their art activity, for
> the most part, takes place outside the conventional exhibi-
> tion parameters of galleries and museums. And it is realized
> that when such artists are asked to participate in the conven-
> tional context of a group exhibition at an established space, it
> is possible that this context can become the controlling fac-
> tor in any individual artist's presentation. Thus it is important

> that the artists asked to participate are interested in furthering
> their concerns within the conventional context.[12]

The installations by Lawler and Piper, in particular, share Rosler's concern with subjectivity and the repositioning of subject and object relationships to uncover politically charged in-between conditions and spaces of contested identities. Lawler's untitled installation included an 1824 painting of a racehorse by Henry Stullman, borrowed from the New York Racing Association. [16, 17] Placed high in front of the windows on a wall dividing two galleries, the painting was flanked by two theatrical spotlights directed not at the painting but at the viewer, interfering with the painting's visibility, and, at night, projecting the viewers' shadows onto the facade of the Citibank across the street. [18, 19] This gesture connected the isolated exhibition space of the gallery with its outside environment, and brought the exhibition to the attention of passersby. In this way, Lawler's installation made the elements of an exhibition the subject of her work—the institutional framework, the autonomy of art production, the processes of artistic commodification, and the physical site. Lawler's installation raised questions of material definition and the spatial displacement of mechanisms of display by radically realigning the relationship between mode of address and audience through the social repositioning of interiority and exteriority. The installation highlighted the diverging subjectivities of the gallery insider "consuming" the artistic experience versus the subjectivity of the everyday person walking down the street.

In a small white alcove separated from the other installations in the exhibition, Adrian Piper installed a 30 by 30 inch black and white photograph behind reflective Plexiglas that depicted black South Africans descending a staircase while staring directly into the camera (and directly at the viewer). [20, 21] The photograph was positioned on the wall such that the viewer was located at its base, while a taped monologue titled *Aspects of the Liberal Dilemma* (read by the artist herself) directly questioned the viewer's reaction to the photograph as well as the viewer's perception. Piper's voice takes the incessant and authoritative tone of a lecturer addressing and informing the viewer:

> It doesn't matter who these people are. They're parts of a
> piece of art, which is part of an art exhibit, in an art gallery,
> in Soho, in New York City. This gallery is one of the best:

progressive, daring, shows some of the most interesting and
aesthetically innovative work around. You expect, and hope
that when you leave this gallery, your conception of what art
can be will be altered, maybe even expanded if only by the
smallest fraction.[13]

Similarly to Lawler, Piper makes the viewer aware of the act of looking at and reading the image. The taped monologue's interrogation
leads the viewer to realize that his or her responses are the primary focus
of the work:

In looking at this picture, you carefully monitor any subliminal
or undisciplined reactions you have to this image of assertive,
aggressive, angry-looking blacks; they might be a part of
the piece. In fact, all your reactions, all your thoughts about
what you're now experiencing might be part of this piece. In
this space, in this gallery, in front of this picture, you don't
want to let your politics interfere with or deaden your aesthetic perceptions, but rather contribute to them: your political
reactions are part of the art experience you are trying to have.
So you try to be extra self-conscious about all your responses
in order to understand the piece better...[14]

While the fundamental concept of the monologue centers on the preconceptions and perceptions of the viewer, the question of race—"assertive,
aggressive, angry-looking blacks"—is brought into the discourse as a result
of the interplay between identity and subjectivity. Furthermore, the monologue's reference to the viewer's politics and interpretations—"What do
these images mean? What's the significance of all the people in the photo
being black? Of they're looking angry or sullen? Of their shabbiness?"—
illustrate the complex and multivalent relationships between concept, subject, object, representation, and racial identity.

Writing in the *Village Voice*, critic April Kingsley wrote that Piper

managed to pull together the erotic, political, socioeconomic,
and aesthetic themes that have long engaged her into a single compelling work...The work as a whole literalizes the old
saw that a work of art questions reality, poses problems, and

challenges previous art. It also ironically plays with the notion that beauty is in the eye of the beholder, since all the
eyes in the piece stare at you, and, in this way, it exemplifies
Duchamp's statement that "the artist is only one aspect
of the creative process. The spectator—by his active
response—completes the cycle." Piper's words, mercifully
spoken out instead of being intoned as is all too common
these days in this kind of "alternate space art," stir up the
voyeuristic implications of view art, and the sexual charge it
may provide when she asks, "What's the point of their seem-
ing to stare at you?" and "Why do you always seem to end
up staring at your own reflection in the glass? At the expression on your face, in your eyes, around your mouth?"[15]

Hence, the viewer is engaged in a visual and spatial tête-à-tête with
the subjects in the photograph and with the artist. This relationship flickers
between spatial foreground, background, and multiple subjectivities.

Piper's exploration of racial identity, representation, and subjectivity was
made still more explicit in *The Mythic Being* (1972–75), a street performance in which she dressed as a man with a dark mustache, afro wig,
and reflective wire rimmed sunglasses. In a related text titled "The Mythic
Being: Getting Back," Piper described this alter ego as a "third-world,
working-class, overtly hostile male."[16] The performances were recorded on
videotape as Piper walked through the streets of New York reciting pas-
sages from her journal. This challenged passersby to classify her through
the lens of their own preconceptions about race, gender, and class. The
video recordings reveal Piper's spatial and programmatic disruptions to
the social and cultural economies of New York street life and urban space,
as passersby and onlookers attempt to decipher Piper's presence and
repeated incoherent mumblings: "*No matter how much I ask my mother to
stop buying crackers, cookies, and things, she does anyway even if I
always eat it; so, I've decided to fast…*"[17] Piper later produced a series of
photographic stills from the performances and annotated the photos with
a philosophical monologue on identity. The images comprise Piper's *I am
the Locus* series (1975), and the resulting images—which appear to be
somewhere between montage and comic drawing—capture the spatialization of subjectivity and identity through techniques of drawing, text, and
erasure that at once dislocate and reposition Piper's own presence and

alternate subjectivity. [22–26] Each photo is annotated with a phrase that floats above the Mythic Being's head:

"I AM THE LOCUS OF CONSCIOUSNESS"
"SURROUNDED AND CONSTRAINED"
"BY ANIMATE PHYSICAL OBJECTS"
"WITH MOIST, FLESHY, PULSATING SURFACES"
"GET OUT OF MY WAY, ASSHOLE"

Perhaps it's no coincidence that the show that took place in Artists Space six months prior to the Reiring group installation was the first major solo exhibition of the architect Bernard Tschumi and the first show of his architectural drawings held in a gallery or a public space. Tschumi's sympathies with these neo-avant-garde artists are notable, in that he sought to radicalize architecture in the 1970s and 1980s not only in terms of procedural operations but also in terms of spatial representation, linguistic tactics, and subject/object spatial identity. The exhibition and installation, *Architectural Manifestos*, included a series of drawings, manifestos, and notations deploying very similar techniques to those of his avant-garde artist contemporaries: "Manifesto 1, Fireworks" (1974); "Manifesto 2, Questions of Space or the Box" (1975); "Manifesto 3, Advertisements for Architecture" (1976); "Manifesto 4, Joyce's Garden" (1977); "Manifesto 5, Birth of an Angel" (1977); "Manifesto 6, The Park" (1977); "Manifesto 7, Border Crossing" (1978); and "Manifesto 8, The Room" (1978).

Tschumi initially moved to New York because he was interested in the art scene and wished to forge connections between neo-avant-garde art and an architectural discourse. "For me at this time it was very important to get involved with the art scene," he later recalled. "I saw it as an escape from the restrictive political dimension of architecture. And I was fascinated by what was happening in New York in the '60s and '70s. So I was coming to New York for the art scene." [18] Tschumi was interested in questioning the idea of what happens in space, the actions of characters in space, and the connections between architecture and disciplines like performance art and film (including the work of Michelangelo Antonioni and, as with Martha Rosler, Jean-Luc Godard).

The relationships between architecture and art were the focus of a special September/October 1975 issue of *Studio International,* a journal of modern art. The issue included essays by Daniel Buren, Germano Celant, RoseLee Goldberg, Dan Graham, Charles Jencks, Joseph Rykwert, and Bernard Tschumi, among others. Of particular note, the essays by Celant, Goldberg, and Tschumi focused on discursive spaces within art and architectural production. In each of these three essays, the concepts of space, spatial relationships, and experience are critical to the making of art and architecture that reorients subject and object relationships in order to address questions of politics and institutional critique, pointing the way towards latent considerations of subjectivity and identity.

In the article "Artspaces," Celant writes:

> Spatial articulation becomes the object of the artist who immerses himself in the space, treating it concretely like material to be molded. He puts it together and organizes it, not only on a superficial and visual level, but also in such a way that it affects the spectator's own senses and movement. The result is something more than a mere projection of surfaces, homologous to the actual walls, it involves a real experience of the given field, with the plastic relationships providing the environment with an extra dimension.[19]

The article includes examples that put *space* rather than *form* into question, such as Kurt Schwitters's *Merzbau* in Hanover (ca. 1927), Alexander Rodchenko's *Line Construction* (ca. 1917), Duchamp's *Door, Il Rue Larrey* (1927), and Vito Acconci's *Voices for a Second Sight* (1974) installation at the Museum of Modern Art in New York.

RoseLee Goldberg's article, "Space as Praxis," begins with the affirmation that space is always inherent in art. The article, which takes as its starting point the February 1975 exhibition and publication of *A Space: A Thousand Words* at the Royal College of Art Gallery in London (which she co-curated with Tschumi), considers the way in which the perception of space is challenged and altered through experience and various spatial praxes. In examining the tensions between theory and practice in the production of art, Goldberg cites the experience of space as the differentiating factor:

> If we think of the ways in which much conceptual art and performance work are presented, it is clear that performance

implies a different kind, i.e. quantity, of space, for its execu-
tion. Space becomes the medium for practice and actual
experience. Put simply then, "theory"—whether "concepts,"
"drawing," or "documentation"—remains essentially two-
dimensional, while "practice performance" implies a physical
context, a space in which to experience the materialization
of that theory.[20]

Goldberg's emphasis on performance space and the materialization of
concepts leads to an insistence on the body as a means of experiencing space and creates a different spatial expression than the painting and
sculpture of previous avant-garde movements.

Goldberg's article precedes and references Tschumi's essay entitled
"Questions of Space: The Pyramid and the Labyrinth (or the Architectural
Paradox)." [27] The front plate to "Questions of Space" includes the follow-
ing caption:

Questions of Space. Experienced (A), Conceived (B),
Perceived (C)

On April 21, 1975, visiting an architectural exhibition in
Central London, I asked 66 viewers to write questions relating to space. This inquiry into the matter formed the question
pattern that defined a "question space," i.e. the first form of
presentation. The viewers' writings defined another space
and provided the second form of presentation. I then set further series of questions and new forms of presentation, one of
which is illustrated here. The numbers refer to the questions
included in the footnotes section of my article. The plan is one
of Palladio's unrealized villas.[21]

Tschumi's article later became the collection of essays entitled *Questions
of Space*, which includes the original article (with its title shortened to
"The Architectural Paradox") along with the entire list of questions posed
by the sixty-six viewers, as well as the seminal essay "The Pleasure of
Architecture." In "The Architectural Paradox," Tschumi acknowledges
the failures of the utopian ideals of the early-twentieth-century architectural
avant-garde, as well as the rupture between utopian ideals and social

realities that gave way to dismay and disillusion with political structures and eventually resulted in the reformulation of architectural concepts by "those who turned towards earlier centuries and advocated restoration and continuity based on historical precedents."[22]

In the *Studio International* article, Tschumi attempts to get at the very nature of architecture itself—space. The article is a conceptual montage of jump-cuts, cross-cuts, and dissolves through experienced, conceived, and perceived space. This montage is constructed through the annotation of the Palladian floor plan with an inset numerical index that refers to the sixty-six viewers and their questions, which are also indexed in a photograph placed above the floor plan; the viewers' questions are then referenced back to the body of the text through footnotes. The article also employs a number of illustrated footnotes, citing a range of art and architecture from Bruce Nauman's *Floating Room* (1974) to Tschumi's own "architectural performance" entitled *Fireworks* (1974). [28] The illustrated footnotes are precursors to the conceptual techniques Tschumi later deploys in the *Advertisements for Architecture* (1976) and the *Manhattan Transcripts* (1981).

Tschumi wrote in 1990 that the aim of the article was a conscious strategy "in parallel to the concerns of critics, philosophers and artists of our time to open up unexplored ground and develop conceptual tools for the making of a new architecture."[23] Furthermore, in the text he characterizes a new split within architectural discourse that emerged from the previous rupture—a split between the ontological form of architecture and the experience of space. Yet, this split is not so cut and dry. For perception and reason cannot be so easily decoupled, and instead operate within a mirror-image relationship oscillating between the subject and object of space:

> In "deprived space," to borrow the terminology of Germano Celant, the "participants" can only find themselves as the subject, aware only of their fantasies and pulsations, able only to react to the signals of their own bodies. The materiality of the body coincides with the materiality of the space. By a series of exclusions that become significant only in opposition to the remote exterior space and social context, the subjects in "deprived space" are able only to "experience their own experience."[24]

The paradox of architecture is not about the impossible reconciliation of perception of the architectural concept and real space but about the complex and dialectical relationship between the "ideal" (form) and the "real" (experience) in architecture—the questioning of the nature of space while at the same time experiencing a real space that is sensual and, perhaps, even political.

In 1976 Tschumi published two of his *Advertisements for Architecture* alongside the essay "Architecture and Transgression" in the journal *Oppositions*. Using Dadaist photomontage techniques with Georges Bataille-like headlines that indicate the sensual, erotic, or even perverse conditions of architecture, Tschumi confronts the prospective consumer's deepest fears of rationalism and reason made manifest in aesthetics. The advertisements emphasize the conception of architectural modernism— idealized, rational, clean, and white—as an agent in the wider social repression of anxieties about cultural and political heterogeneity and "otherness." The advertisements that concern Villa Savoye, Le Corbusier's most recognizable project which had since entered a state of decay, is promoted as the ultimate erotic object caught between sensuality and rationalism, revealing both the "traces of reason" and the "sensual experience of space." [29, 30] In particular, the first of the two advertisements argues: "Architecture only survives where it negates the form that society expects of it. Where it negates itself by transgressing the limits that history has set for it." [25]

The publication of the *Advertisements for Architecture* parallels the strategies of appropriation, dissociation of subject and object, and redirection in Rosler, Lawler, Piper, and other artists such as Barbara Kruger and Jenny Holzer, where the languages of advertising, television, photography, and the ideology of everyday experience were subject to formal and linguistic operations. One might detect in this the model of Roland Barthes, whose semiotic analyses were intended to deconstruct hegemonic ideologies. As Benjamin Buchloh writes, "Barthes' strategy of secondary mythification repeats the semiotic and linguistic devaluation of primary language by myth and structurally follows [Walter] Benjamin's ideas on the allegorical procedure that reiterates the devaluation of the object by commoditization." [26] Likewise, Tschumi used language and the techniques of advertising and photography to transgress architecture's ideologies. Reflecting upon the 1978 *Architectural Manifestos* exhibition at Artists

Space, Tschumi stated in 1998, "I felt in many ways the art context
was an incredible one in which to push the boundaries and limits of
architecture and to explore areas you cannot in the context of normal architectural practice."[27]

While the concepts of subjectivity and identity were never made explicit
in Tschumi's writings and architectural projects, the strategies and operations deployed by neo-avant-garde artists and by Tschumi's own writerly
and exhibitionary practice have much to say about how those subjectivities
and identities are constructed and perceived. Tschumi's focus on spatial
experience indirectly extends outward to encompass forms of subjectivity,
as there is a profound relationship between experience and self. This con-
nection can be seen in the writings of Jacques Lacan and Michel Foucault.
The Lacanian psychoanalytic subject is constituted through a perceptual
and spatial process of differentiation (the mirror stage), whereby the subject and object engage in a fluctuating relationship of the gaze. On the
other hand, the Foucauldian subject is constituted historically in its relation to forms of power and social practices in his early writings, and in later
writings this subject is self-constituted and self-reflexive within a framework
of discursive practices. The shift in Foucault's conception of the subject
occurs between the first volume of his *History of Sexuality* (in which the
subject is dominated by the sexual repression of seventeenth century bourgeois order) and the final two volumes of *History of Sexuality* (Vol. 2, *The
Use of Pleasure* and Vol. 3, *The Care of the Self*), in which he arrives at
a strategy of "aesthetics of existence" designed to practice power over the
self by the self.[28] Likewise, Tschumi attempted to liberate architecture from
its historical repressive powers through his architectural operations and
Bataillean strategies.

Foucault's project on the self culminated in his faculty seminar on
"Technologies of the Self" presented at the University of Vermont in the fall
of 1982. The seminar began an investigation of the praxes used by subjects, by their own means or through the aid of others to act on their own
body, soul, thought, conduct, and manner in order to attain a particular
state of being. In the resulting book *Technologies of the Self* (1988), published after Foucault's death in 1984, he sets out a genealogy of how the
self constituted itself as subject. In his examination of Plato's *Alcibiades I*,
Foucault analyzes the notion of "taking care of oneself" as the intersection
of political ambition and philosophical love. Furthermore, in the translation

from the Greek word *Epimelesthai,* "taking care of oneself" expresses more than the simplicity of paying attention; more specifically it refers to "taking pains with oneself" and one's health. "Taking pains with oneself" is then divided into the following questions: "What is this self of which one has to take care, and of what does that care consists?"

> First, what is the self? Self is a reflexive pronoun, and it has two meanings. Auto means "the same," but it also conveys the notion of identity. The latter meaning shifts the question from "What is this self?" to "What is the plateau on which I shall find my identity?"[29]

Foucault's analysis is not intended to suggest that identity is predetermined, but rather, identity can be located within a spatial construct or within the spatial relationships through which subjectivity is constituted as the result of experience and reflexivity.

It has been frequently assumed that architectural space is incapable of locating identity and its accompanying politics. After all, modernism's failure to adequately confront the social realities and ills of urban life in the 1960s and 1970s are well rehearsed, and identity politics were thought to be better left to artists' two-dimensional representations. The architectural projects of modernism—housing projects and otherwise—did not address the subjectivities of their users or inhabitants, but rather projected paternalistic views of their subjects through the abject lenses of poverty, class, and race. In contrast, the discursive spaces of neo-avant-garde artists like Rosler, Lawler, and Piper, and the architectural transgressions of Tschumi, reveal both the construction of subjectivity and the multivalent spatial relationships through which those subjectivities are formed. The operations they deployed—spatially connecting visual foregrounds with their political and cultural backgrounds, the social repositioning of relationships of interiority and exteriority, visual and spatial flickering between the "other" and its repressive power structure, and programmatic and spatial disruptions to normative hierarchies of architecture and urban space—do not portend a set of codified techniques for rendering identity in architecture. Rather, these actions inform the possibilities for locating and revealing identity within architectural space and its relationships. Concepts are materialized through the experience of space that in turn renders identity through the interactions of multiple subjectivities. Hence, questions of space and experience translate into questions of identity, and such discursive spaces have the power to reveal cultural, political, sexual, ethnic, and even black identity.

NOTES

1. Peter Burger, *Theory of the Avant-Garde*, trans. Michael Shaw (Minneapolis: University of Minnesota Press, 1984), 58.

2. Burger, *Theory of the Avant-Garde*, 60.

3. Hal Foster, "What's Neo about the Neo-Avant-Garde?" in *October* 70, "The Duchamp Effect" (Autumn 1994): 23–25.

4. Burger, *Theory of the Avant-Garde*, 61. See also Benjamin H.D. Buchloh's discussion of Burger's lack of awareness of late 1960's and early 1970's artists whose work radically opposed the "institutionalization of the avant-garde as art" in "The Primary Colors for the Second Time: A Paradigm Repetition of the Neo-Avant-Garde," *October* 37 (Summer 1986): 42.

5. Hans Richter, *Dada: Art and Anti-Art*, trans. David Britt (New York and Toronto: Oxford University Press, 1965), 116. Originally published as Hans Richter, *Dada, Kunst und Antikunst.*

6. George Grosz's account of the invention of photomontage is quoted in Richter, *Dada, Art and Anti-Art*, 117. See also Benjamin H.D. Buchloh, "Allegorical Procedures: Appropriation and Montage in Contemporary Art," *Artforum*, vol. 21, no. 1 (September 1982): 43. Finally, see Dawn Ades, *Photomontage* (London: Thames and Hudson, 1976), 12–18. Grosz disputes Raoul Hausmann's claim to have been the inventor of photomontage. Richter offers Hausmann's version of the invention of photomontage also in *Art and Anti-Art*. Hausmann's quote is taken from *Definition der Foto-Montage* (Definition of Photmontage): "The Dadaists, who had 'invented' static simultaneous and phonetic poetry applied the same principles to visual representation. They were the first to use photography to create, from often totally disparate spatial and material elements, a new unity in which was revealed a visually and conceptually new image of chaos of an age and revolution. And they were aware that their method possessed a power for propaganda purposes which their contemporaries had not the courage to exploit." See Richter, *Dada, Art and Anti-Art*, 116.

7. Raoul Hausmann, "Fotomontage," in *A-Z* 16 (May 1931). Reprinted in *Raoul Hausmann* (Hanover: Keslnergesellschaft, 1981), 51; translated by Buchloh in "Allegorical Procedures," 43.

8. Buchloh, "Allegorical Procedures," 44.

9. Buchloh, "Allegorical Procedures," 44.

10. Taken from an interview with Martha Rosler by Laura Cottingham for the catalog essay, "The War is Always Home: Martha Rosler," in *Bringing the War Home: Photomontages from the Vietnam War Era* (New York: Simon Watson Gallery, October 1991). *House Beautiful: Bringing the War Home* is the original title of the

series which was subsequently reversed in a number of publications. The artist has since repaired the circulating title of the series of photomontages in question.

11. Cottingham, "The War is Always Home."

12. Janelle Reiring, *The Proposal for Artists Space* (New York: Artists Space, 1978).

13. Monica E. McTighe, *Framed Spaces: Photography and Memory in Contemporary Installation Art* (Hanover, NH: Dartmouth College Press, 2012), 62. See also the 5:33 minute audio monologue at the Adrian Piper Research Archive (ARPA) at www.adrianpiper.com. A second version of the installation was installed at the Wadsworth Atheneum, Museum of Art in Hartford, Connecticut, March 7 through April 6, 1980.

14. Adrian Piper, *Aspects of the Liberal Dilemma* (1978), audio monologue, Adrian Piper Research Archive (ARPA), www.adrianpiper.com.

15. April Kingsley, "Art Goes Underground," *The Village Voice,* October 16, 1978, 122.

16. Adrian Piper, "The Mythic Being: Getting Back," in *Out of Order, Out of Sight: Selected Writings in Meta-Art, 1968–1992* (Cambridge, MA: MIT Press, 1999), 147.

17. Excerpted from the film *Other Than Art's Sake* by the Australian artist Peter Kennedy, which documents Adrian Piper's *Mythic Being* street performances. The film includes footage of Piper getting into and out of drag, rehearsing her mantra taken from her journal, and roaming the streets muttering it, followed by crowds of curious onlookers. *Other Than Art's Sake* also includes work by and interviews with Ian Breakwell, Judy Chicago and Arlene Raven, Hans Haacke, David Medalla, Charles Simonds, and Stephen Willats.

18. Joan Ockman, "Talking with Bernard Tschumi," *Log* 13/14 (2008): 163.

19. Germano Celant, "Artspaces," *Studio International: Journal of Modern Art,* vol. 190, no. 977 (September/October 1975): 116.

20. RoseLee Goldberg, "Space as Praxis," *Studio International: Journal of Modern Art,* vol. 190, no. 977 (September/October 1975): 130.

21. Bernard Tschumi, "Questions of Space: The Pyramid and the Labyrinth (or the Architectural Paradox)," *Studio International: Journal of Modern Art,* vol. 190, no. 977 (September/October 1975): 136. Tschumi would later reveal that he was surprised when the article turned up in architecture schools.

22. Bernard Tschumi, *Questions of Space* (London: Architectural Association, 1990), 8.

23. Tschumi, *Questions of Space*, 9.

24. Tschumi, *Questions of Space*, 140.

25. Bernard Tschumi, "Architecture and Transgression," *Oppositions* 7 (Winter 1976–77), 56.

26. Buchloh, "Allegorical Procedures," 47.

27. Claudia Gould and Valerie Smith, eds., *5000 Artists Return to Artists Space: 25 Years* (New York: Artists Space, 1998), 95.

28. See Andrew Thacker's discussion in "Foucault's Aesthetics of Existence," in *Radical Philosophy* 63 (Spring 1993), 13.

29. Luther Martin, Huck Gutman, and Patrick H. Hutton, eds., *Technologies of the Self: A Seminar With Michel Foucault* (Amherst: The University of Massachusetts Press, 1988), 25.

1.

1.
LUDOVICO CARRACCI
*LA MADONNA COL BAMBINO FRA I SANTI GIUSEPPE,
FRANCESCO ED I COMMITTENTI* ("*LA CARRACINA*").
PINACOTECA CIVICA, CENTO, 1591.

2.

2.
CARAVAGGIO
THE RAISING OF LAZARUS, MUSEO REGIONALE,
MESSINA, C.1609.

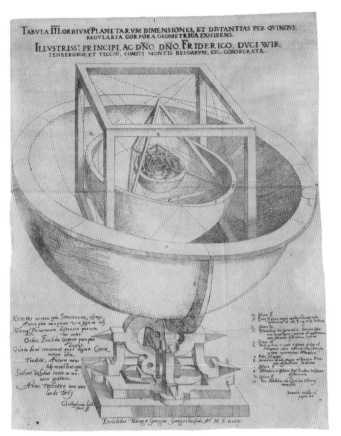

3.

3.
JOHANNES KEPLER
MYSTERIUM COSMOGRAPHICUM, 1596.

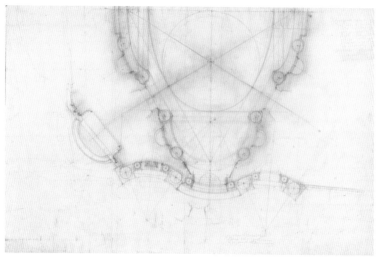

4.

5.

4–5.
FRANCESCO BORROMINI
SAN CARLO ALLE QUATTRO FONTANE, ROME, 1638–41; PLAN DRAWING AND
INTERIOR VIEW.

6.

6.
FRANCESCO BORROMINI
ST. IVO DELLA SAPIENZA, ROME, 1642–60; PLAN DRAWING.

7.

7.
FRANCESCO BORROMINI
ST. IVO DELLA SAPIENZA, ROME, 1642–60; INTERIOR VIEW OF DOME.

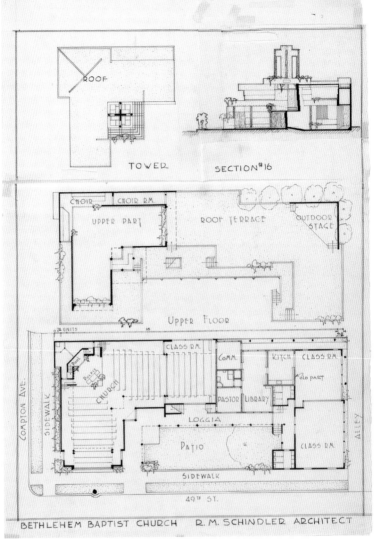

ROOF

TOWER   SECTION #16

CHOIR   CHOIR RM.

UPPER PART   ROOF TERRACE   OUTDOOR STAGE

UPPER FLOOR

CLASS RM.   COMM.   KITCH   CLASS RM.
                                old part
CHURCH
                 PASTOR LIBRARY
COMPTON AVE
SIDEWALK   LOGGIA
         PATIO   CLASS RM.
                                      ALLEY
         SIDEWALK
              49ᵗʰ ST.

BETHLEHEM BAPTIST CHURCH   R. M. SCHINDLER ARCHITECT

8.

8.
R.M. SCHINDLER
BETHLEHEM BAPTIST CHURCH, LOS ANGELES, CALIFORNIA, 1944; SITE PLAN,
FLOOR PLAN, ROOF PLAN, AND ELEVATION.

9.

10.

9–10.
R.M. SCHINDLER
BETHLEHEM BAPTIST CHURCH, LOS ANGELES, CALIFORNIA, 1944; EXTERIOR
VIEW FROM SOUTH COMPTON AVENUE AND INTERIOR VIEW. PHOTOGRAPHS
BY JULIUS SHULMAN, 1944.

11.

12.

11.
R.M. SCHINDLER
BETHLEHEM BAPTIST CHURCH, LOS ANGELES, CALIFORNIA, 1944; EXTERIOR VIEW
FROM SOUTH COMPTON AVENUE. PHOTOGRAPH BY JULIUS SHULMAN.

12.
R.M. SCHINDLER AND THEODORE DREISER LOOKING AT A BLUEPRINT
OF THE BETHLEHEM BAPTIST CHURCH, CIRCA 1944.
PHOTOGRAPHER UNKNOWN.

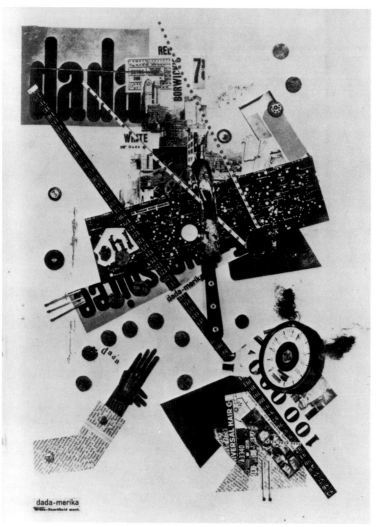

13.

GEORGE GROSZ AND JOHN HEARTFIELD
DADA-MERIKA, 1919; PHOTOMONTAGE. COLLECTION PAUL CITROEN.

14.

14.
MARTHA ROSLER
RED STRIPE KITCHEN, FROM THE SERIES *HOUSE BEAUTIFUL: BRINGING THE WAR HOME*, C. 1967–72; PHOTOMONTAGE.

15.

15.
MARTHA ROSLER
CLEANING THE DRAPES, FROM THE SERIES *HOUSE BEAUTIFUL: BRINGING THE WAR HOME*, CIRCA 1967–72; PHOTOMONTAGE.

16.

17.

16–17.
LOUISE LAWLER
INSTALLATION AT ARTISTS SPACE, SEPTEMBER 1978; INSTALLATION VIEWS.

18.

19.

18–19.
LOUISE LAWLER
INSTALLATION AT ARTISTS SPACE, SEPTEMBER 1978; INSTALLATION VIEW OF
SILHOUETTES IN WINDOW AND PROJECTION ACROSS STREET.

20.

20.
ADRIAN PIPER
ASPECTS OF THE LIBERAL DILEMMA, ARTISTS SPACE, SEPTEMBER 1978;
INSTALLATION VIEW.

21.

21.
ADRIAN PIPER
ASPECTS OF THE LIBERAL DILEMMA, SEPTEMBER 1978; DETAIL OF INSTALLATION
PHOTOGRAPH, BERKELEY ART MUSEUM, BERKELEY, CALIFORNIA.

22.

25.

23.

26.

24.

22–26.
ADRIAN PIPER
I AM THE LOCUS (#1–5), 1975; OIL CRAYON DRAWING ON PHOTOGRAPH.
DAVID AND ALFRED SMART MUSEUM OF ART, THE UNIVERSITY OF CHICAGO.

1.2   3.42   1.3   2.51   1.6113 1.7   2.61   2.63   4.3   1.731

··· A

1. 1.1 1.2 1.21 1.22 1.221 1.23
1.3 1.4 1.41 1.411 1.412 1.5
1.6 1.61 1.611   1.6111 1.6112
1.6113 1.6114 1.6115 1.6116 1.7
1.7 1.71 1.72 1.73 1.731 2. 2.1
2.2 2.21 2.3 2.4 2.4 2.5 2.51
2.52 2.6 2.61 2.61 2.612 2.62
2.63 2.64 2.65 2.7 2.71 2.7 2.8
2.81 2.9 3. 3.1 3.11 3.12 3.2
3.21 3.3 3.31 3.4 3.41 3.42 3.5
3.51 4. 4.1 4.2 4.2 4.21 4.22
4.221 4.23 4.3 4.4 4.5 4.5 4.6
4.7 4.7 4.8 4.81 4.811

··· B

1.611

··· C

3.41
3.51
4
4.221
4.4

4.21

1.6115   2.62
1.731   2.64
2.3   2.65
2.52   2.7
2.61   2.72

1.6111   1.6113

1.23   2.612   1.22   2.81
2.6

Questions of Space. Experienced (A), Conceived (B), Perceived (C)

On April 21, 1975, visiting an architectural exhibition in Central London, I asked 66 viewers to write questions relating to space. This inquiry into the matter formed the question pattern that defined a 'question space', i.e. the first form of presentation. The viewers' writings defined another space and provided the second form of presentation. I then set further series of questions and new forms of presentation, one of which is illustrated here. The numbers refer to the questions included in the footnotes section of my article. The plan is one of Palladio's unrealized villas.

27.

27.
BERNARD TSCHUMI
FRONT PLATE ILLUSTRATION FOR "QUESTIONS OF SPACE: THE PYRAMID AND THE
LABYRINTH (OR THE PARADOX OF ARCHITECTURE)," 1975.

28.

28.
BERNARD TSCHUMI
FRONT PLATE ILLUSTRATION FOR "QUESTIONS OF SPACE: THE PYRAMID AND THE
LABYRINTH (OR THE PARADOX OF ARCHITECTURE)," 1975.

The most architectural thing about this building is the state of decay in which it is.

VILLA SAVOYE, 1965

Architecture only survives
where it negates the form that
society expects of it.
Where it negates itself by
transgressing the limits that
history has set for it.

29.

29–30.
BERNARD TSCHUMI
VILLA SAVOYE (ADVERTISEMENTS FOR ARCHITECTURE), 1976–77.

Sensuality has been known to overcome even the most rational of buildings.

VILLA SAVOYE, 1965

Architecture is the ultimate erotic act.
Carry it to excess and it will reveal
both the traces of reason and the sensual
experience of space. Simultaneously.

30.

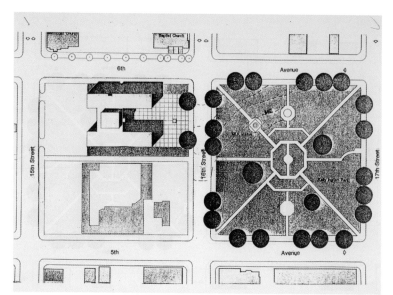

31.

31.
MAX BOND, JR.
BIRMINGHAM CIVIL RIGHTS INSTITUTE, BIRMINGHAM, ALABAMA, 1992;
PRELIMINARY 1986 DESIGN STUDY.

32.

33.

32.
MAX BOND, JR.
BIRMINGHAM CIVIL RIGHTS INSTITUTE, BIRMINGHAM, ALABAMA, 1992; VIEW NEAR
COVERED WALKWAY TOWARDS THE 16TH STREET BAPTIST CHURCH.

33.
MAX BOND, JR.
BIRMINGHAM CIVIL RIGHTS INSTITUTE, BIRMINGHAM, ALABAMA, 1992;
PRESENT-DAY SATELLITE VIEW.

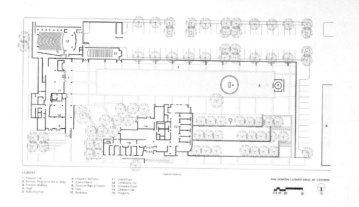

34.

34.
MAX BOND, JR.
MARTIN LUTHER KING JR. CENTER FOR NONVIOLENT SOCIAL CHANGE IN ATLANTA,
GEORGIA, 1982; GROUND FLOOR PLAN.

35.

36.

35–36.
MAX BOND, JR.
MARTIN LUTHER KING JR. CENTER FOR NONVIOLENT SOCIAL CHANGE IN
ATLANTA, GEORGIA, 1982; VIEW FROM COVERED PASSAGE TOWARDS
THE KING MEMORIAL AND VIEW FROM THE CHAPEL OF ALL FAITHS TOWARDS THE
KING MEMORIAL. PHOTOGRAPH BY GORDON H. SCHENCK, JR. ARCHITECTURAL
AND ENGINEERING PHOTOGRAPHY.

37.

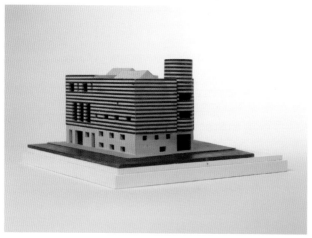

38.

37.
ADOLF LOOS, VILLA MÜLLER, PRAGUE, 1930; VIEW OF ENTRANCE.

38.
ADOLF LOOS, HOUSE FOR JOSEPHINE BAKER, 1927–28; MODEL.

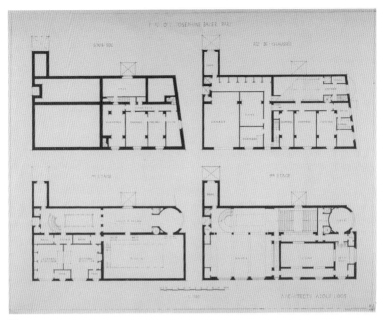

39.

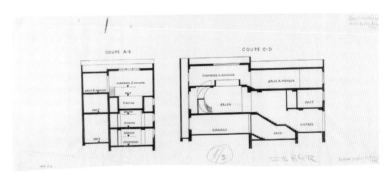

40.

39–40.
ADOLF LOOS, HOUSE FOR JOSEPHINE BAKER, 1927–28; PLAN
AND SECTION DRAWINGS.

41.

41.
PORTRAIT OF MISS AMAZA LEE MEREDITH, UNDATED.
PHOTOGRAPHER UNKNOWN.

42.

43.

42–43.
AMAZA LEE MEREDITH
AZUREST SOUTH, CHESTERFIELD COUNTY, VIRGINIA, 1939; NORTHEAST
ELEVATION AND INTERIOR VIEW OF LIVING ROOM.

44.

44.
AMAZA LEE MEREDITH
AZUREST SOUTH, CHESTERFIELD COUNTY, VIRGINIA, 1939; INTERIOR VIEW.

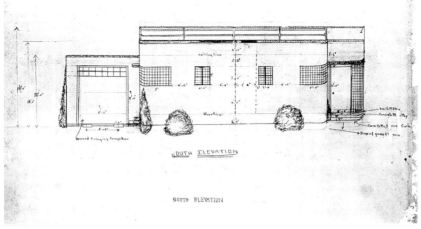

SOUTH ELEVATION

SOUTH ELEVATION

45.

46.

45–46.
AMAZA LEE MEREDITH
AZUREST SOUTH, CHESTERFIELD COUNTY, VIRGINIA, 1939; SOUTH ELEVATION
DRAWING AND EXTERIOR VIEW.

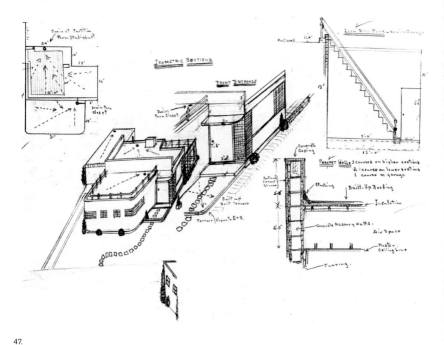

47.

47.
AMAZA LEE MEREDITH
AZUREST SOUTH, CHESTERFIELD COUNTY, VIRGINIA, 1939; SOUTH ELEVATION
ISOMETRIC SECTION.

THE PROBLEM WITH
AFRICAN AMERICAN MUSEUMS

How does it feel to be a problem? This question exemplifies the struggle for social justice that opens W.E.B. Du Bois's *The Souls of Black Folk*, a book of essays that delves into the question of "The Negro Problem"—the place of the Negro in American society. As black Americans have sought to define that place over the past decades, they have variously been labeled "negro," "colored," "black," and now "African American." That the phrase "African American" is used to describe Americans of African ancestry (the majority of whose ancestors were not immigrants to the United States, but rather were forcibly removed from their native lands and sold into slavery in Colonial America until the early nineteenth century) as well as to identify cultural production by black Americans is a recognition of the double consciousness of being both black and American. According to Du Bois, the black American is born with a veil and gifted with second-sight in a world that yields him no true self-consciousness and in which he only sees himself through the revelation of the otherworld. "It is a peculiar sensation, this double-consciousness," writes Du Bois, "this sense of always looking at one's self through the eyes of others, of measuring one's soul by the tape of a world that looks on in amused contempt and pity. One ever feels his two-ness—An American, a Negro; two souls, two thoughts, two unreconciled strivings; two warring ideals in one dark body, whose dogged strength alone keeps it from being torn asunder." [1]

Yet black Americans have generally resisted the lenses of others' eyes in constructing self-consciousness, rather than merging the two selves. This resistance manifested itself in the New Negro Movement of the 1920s and 1930s, of which Du Bois was the preeminent Negro figure, as well the Black Power Movement of the late 1960s and 1970s. The New Negro Movement gave rise to the Harlem Renaissance, jazz, and the work of such artists and literary figures as Aaron Douglas, Zora Neale Hurston, Countee Cullen, and Langston Hughes. The Black Power Movement resulted in the replacement of the fraught word "Negro" with a celebration of blackness, embodied in the words of James Brown's "Say It Loud, I'm Black and I'm Proud" as well as the profusion of visual symbols like dashikis, Afro hairstyles, and raised fists. Wherever they are situated within this interchange of "double consciousness" and its resistance, black Americans have always been keenly aware of the potency of visual and rhetorical forms in the construction of self-identity.

Likewise, America has always been keenly conscious of black Americans, and across the history of the struggle for racial justice, forms of black self-awareness seeped into the more broadly American cultural consciousness. While early jazz may have been referred to as "race music," the novels of James Baldwin and Richard Wright derisively termed "protest literature," and later rhythm and blues recordings categorized as "race records," today the words "African American" are not used to identify jazz, rhythm and blues, or hip-hop (each of which has been adopted by a multiracial, if still predominantly black, cadre of artists). Nor do the words "African American" inevitably precede the descriptions of works by such poets and writers as Maya Angelou, Toni Morrison, or Alice Walker. But this naturalization of blackness into American culture—resulting in a more postmodern black double consciousness that finds itself at the center of cultural production while still marked by difference—did not bring about the merged, singular, and "better and truer self" that Du Bois described the American Negro longing for.[2] This black consciousness is embedded in the cultural expression of these works not in style or image, but rather in the manner in which these works exist in relationship to all other modes of American cultural production. While the most expected kinds of artistic encounter may rely on opposition or confrontation, the embedded cultural relationships of African American forms like music and literature also exploit paradox, irony, subversion, and nuance. Thus, the double consciousness continues to exist as a condition of being that is communicated in the work and translated through language, meter, syncopation, manner, and self-consciousness.

This expression of black self-awareness within American consciousness has not fully extended to black visual arts and architecture. Perhaps the gaze of mainstream culture (conditioned by centuries of white representation) is not yet able to shift focus from a concept of difference marked by racial otherness and its visual attributes. The prioritization of vision is, after all, the keystone of the modern observer's perception of art, space, and cultural difference. In European art and philosophy, this extends from the sixteenth century with the development of perspectival space and a lineage of religious paintings that emphasized a theological understanding of space—that "seeing is believing." More recently, we have seen that primacy of vision reiterated in Lacan's theory of the gaze and his idea of the "mirror stage," the moment when a child—presumably white, male, and European—is able to distinguish his reflected image in a mirror and differentiate himself from the things around him. Perhaps the forms of self-awareness more common to music and literature have not yet inflected black visual arts and architecture in the consciousness of the casual

observer because the black viewer seeks the recognition of his own reflected image in a mirror stage that for most had been suppressed and
denied for nearly three centuries.

In *Exhibiting Blackness: African Americans and the American Art
Museum*, Bridget Cooks argues that "regardless of the intentions of the
curators, exhibitions of art by African Americans are often perceived
through the limiting 'either/or' paradigm; through a lens of either anthropological study or aesthetic value." The anthropological gaze reflects curiosity
toward the presence of otherness, and the "objective" distancing implicit
in this curiosity confirms an age-old power structure of white cultural superiority and a desire to maintain a hierarchy under which Black culture is
viewed as inferior. The aesthetic gaze, by contrast, presents art by African
Americans—which historically has been absent and misrepresented in mainstream art museums—as being devoid of cultural context, objects to be
appreciated for their representational or textural inventiveness but little else.
As a rejoinder to these defaults, Cooks argues instead for exhibitions that
"demonstrate the understanding of artistic merit and Black identity as in-
terdependent instead of mutually exclusive categories." She continues that
because exhibitions have pedagogical roles—teaching the values of art,
cultures, social movements, and national histories—exhibition spaces are
inevitably contested spaces for African Americans, a population whose
presence in those histories is highly complex. The visiting public internalizes
these institutional narratives of cultural history and art history, making the
museum gallery a critical space for black representation and participation.[3]

The museum building itself is likewise a contested typology for African
Americans, thanks not only to the historical absence of art by African
Americans but also the history of segregation and Jim Crow laws that pre-
vented the presence of African Americans in certain museums, as well
as the generally complex relationships in American history between race,
space, and cultural identity. Hence, the conditions of this contestation
problematize both the anthropological and aesthetic approaches that enter
into the design of museums for African American art, history, and culture.
These highly loaded acts of architecture require thoughtful consideration of
the multivalencies and complexities of relationships that persist, demanding
more than just a higher aesthetic quality. Such museums need to interrogate more than what can be seen on the surface.

While architecture certainly does overlap with the visual arts and
the production of perspectival space, the current preoccupation with the

image of architecture and its superficial aesthetics—its surfaces, skins, symbols, and skin color—is a recent and postmodern phenomenon, and one that afflicts a number of major African American museums. Furthermore, instead of only serving as a form of remediation for the past injustices of exclusion (and thus the remediation of a perceived "problem"), these museums should also engage questions of cultural identity, social and racial justice, and American identity as a contemporary discourse. Museums are institutions that can and should participate in the work of constructing better understandings of these issues. As such, their architecture should become a form of knowledge rather than displaying the knowledge of form, tropes, and superficial "africanisms" and token symbols of a mythologized African heritage.

Superficialities and generalizations regarding cultural identity usually play out through the constructions of stereotypes. Racist stereotypes of black Americans have long been part of a political and economic equation in American society that places whites on the plus side and blacks on the minus side of the calculations. These stereotypes essentialize blacks as Other and set up an "us versus them" opposition between whites and blacks, in which blacks are perceived as "not like us," not American, not of the same shared history. The "othering" of blacks denies them the right to American history (unless accompanied by the qualifying prefix "African")—a historical and social exorcism. But white and black Americans have a complicated and shared history of intermingled bloodlines, black mammies nursing white babies, and the fact that the American economic system was built on the backs of black slave labor and their inventions—not to mention that political symbols like the U.S. Capitol and the White House were literally built by black slaves. Because of this joint history, white stereotypes of blacks have been constructed to deny to themselves their own blurred blackness.[4] Elisabeth Bronfen has stated that the "stereotype of the Other is used to control the ambivalent and to create boundaries. Stereotypes are a way of dealing with the instabilities arising from the division between self and non-self by preserving an illusion of control and order."[5]

Stereotyping and constructing Otherness are strategies of symbolic containment and risk. That which they seek to resolve into steadfast fixity is, by that move, potentially reanimated as the threat that such strategies wish to keep constantly at bay. Furthermore, as Michael Pickering has written:

> Stereotyping may operate as a way of imposing a sense of
> order on the social world in the same way as categories,
> but with the crucial difference that stereotyping attempts to
> deny any flexible thinking with categories. It denies this in the
> interests of the structures of power that it upholds. It attempts
> to maintain these structures as they are, or to realign them
> in the face of a perceived threat. The comfort of inflexibility
> which stereotypes provides reinforces the conviction that ex-
> isting relations of power are necessary and fixed.[6]

White stereotypes of black Americans—"Sambo," "Mammy," the hypersexulized "Mandingo," and the 1990s "Welfare Queen," among oth- ers—were intended to maintain an image of blacks as servile, illiterate, mentally inferior, lazy but over-sexed, incapable of self-care, and burden- some to American society. Such stereotypes are discriminatory, and are frequently reiterated with the intention of maintaining white power struc- tures and social hierarchies, as well as to induce a fear of black Americans at a time when black political power, visibility in mainstream popular culture, and intellectual discourse have in fact brought about tremendous social change in recent decades. As black Americans have ascended the rungs of social progress, such stereotypes are reminders to keep blacks in check, to "keep them in their place."

The instrumental power of stereotypes makes the self-stereotyping of black culture all the more ironic. This tendency can be seen in the con- sciously Afrocentric symbols of kente cloth, Ashante stools, head-wraps, and occasional Egyptian iconography, each of which aims to fix a definition of what it means to be African American while seeking to recuperate the power of "Africa" as the majestic foundation of much of modern Western civilization. "Afrocentrism, a contemporary species of black nationalism, is a gallant yet misguided attempt to define an African identity in a white so- ciety perceived to be hostile," as Cornel West has written. "It is gallant because it puts black doings and sufferings, not white anxieties and fears, at the center of discussion. It is misguided because—out of fear of cultural hybridization and through silence on the issue of class, retrograde views on black women, gay men, and lesbians, and a reluctance to link race to the common good—it reinforces the narrow discussions about race."[7] The fur- ther irony is that Afrocentrism assumes that everything descended from Africa is homogenous, as if Africa represents a single ethnic group or a single country—the very same critique that is often leveled against the white European colonialists and empire builders who raped the African continent, exploited its resources, and devalued its diversity and the heterogeneity of African cultures.

The problems with social constructions like these go beyond their frequent racism. Whether from the white or black perspective, stereotypes like these lead not to fixity and order but to simplemindedness—one of the prime dangers of lowest-common-denominator thinking in a society that privileges image over idea in politics, popular culture, and mass media. Likewise, the use of cultural stereotypes in architecture reduces a building to the flatness of its two-dimensional representation (image); a sound-bite or "one-liner" figurative symbol (metaphor); or an overused idea, depleted of its original intensity, uncritical, and no longer contributing anything new to the discourse of architecture (cliché).

Stereotypes have at times been deployed in the name of creating counterimages to the prevailing stereotypes of blacks. In a conscious effort to create an alternative image for the Black Power Movement—which emphasized black racial pride, black political and economic power, and the creation of black cultural institutions—many of its radicals began wearing African-styled dashikis, natural rather than processed hair, Afros, and kufis (brimless, short, round skullcap often knitted, crocheted, or made of kente cloth or mud-cloth). A 1969 New York Times "Report on Men's Wear," illustrated with black male models wearing dashikis and Afros standing in front of artwork with African motifs, described the dashiki as a "freedom garment" found neither in Webster's New World Dictionary nor at Brooks Brothers. Designed, manufactured, and sold in Harlem by a company called New Breed, the dashiki's fabrics "may be plain, or in sharp and soft plaids, stripes, and loud prints, or they may be synthetic 'African' such as fake leopard fur. The only authentic African material they use is gold kente braid from Ghana." The article continues matter-of-factly and without irony to add that New Breed's "'African prints' are imported from Holland."

Dashikis quickly moved beyond the world of radical politics to be worn by black celebrities such as Jim Brown and Wilt Chamberlain, and featured in Hollywood movies such as Uptight and Putney Swope, a satire about race in Hollywood films and white-privileging power structures. Kufis were also worn by black entertainers; Marvin Gaye was frequently depicted in one (on the cover of Let's Get It On, for example). This counter-image saw many reflections in black popular culture in television shows such as Soul

Train and *Good Times*, and Afros became a popular hairstyle among a large percentage of black Americans. But these counter-images had limits to their efficacy. The *New York Times* article continues:

> One problem New Breed faces is that while there is a definite interest in Afro dress, encouraged by a lot of black power publicity generated among young people during the school crisis in New York, there is an equally strong interest in turning off the attention and getting back to normal life…. Charles Moore, a Lenox Terrace resident who is regional representative for the education and training division of Volt Information Services Corporation, has a dashiki but says he wouldn't wear it to work. "In this atmosphere it would still be somewhat avant-garde. But I see a lot more people in them on weekends, people who wouldn't go without a shirt ever before."… Kathy Aldrich, fashion editor of the Amsterdam News, thinks that the movement is faddish. "It will start to disappear in a year or two, but it won't go away lightly. There has to be a drastic change in social patterns between the races."[8]

While cultivated counterstereotypes may have helped produce a new subjectivity among black Americans, these final statements inherently raise the question of whether image alone has the agency to change not only social patterns but also relationships of political and economic power, as well as social and cultural relationships—all of which are multidimensional and interrelated. Self-identity extends beyond the two-dimensional surface of the mirror. This problem also extends to the use of Afrocentric imagery in the architecture of African American cultural institutions.

In his well-known analysis of Velázquez's *Las Meninas* (The Maids of Honor), Michel Foucault exposes the spatial tensions embedded within subject-object relationships, as well as the complex web of subjectivities that are constructed through the gazes of the figures in the painting but also those gazes that pass between the viewer of the painting in front of the frame and the painter within the frame. While Foucault's discussion is specific to this single painting and its cast of characters (particularly in his detailed geometric analysis), it also produces a far larger discourse around identity and the blurred boundaries between positions of power, subjectivity, and cultural representation.

At the far end of the room, ignored by all, the unexpected mirror holds in its glow the figures that the painter is looking at (the painter in his represented, objective reality, the reality of the painter at his work); but also the figures that are looking at the painter (in that material reality which the lines and the colors have laid out upon the canvas). These two groups of figures are both equally inaccessible, but in different ways: the first because of an effect of composition peculiar to the painting; the second because of the law that presides over the very existence of all pictures in general. Here, the action of representation consists in bringing one of these two forms of invisibility into the place of the other, in an unstable super-imposition - and in rendering them both, at the same moment, at the other extremity of the picture- at that pole which is the very height of its representation: that of a reflected depth in the far recess of the painting's depth. The mirror provides a metathesis of visibility that affects both the space represented in the picture and its nature as representation; it allows us to see, in the centre of the canvas, what in the painting is of ne-cessity doubly invisible.[9]

Hence, the doubleness of this condition—produced by multiple subjectivi-ties flickering between foreground/background, interior/exterior, and here/there—reveals multiple identities: cultural (the painter Velázquez); political (the royal couple Philip IV and Mariana of Austria); class and labor (two la-dies-in-waiting); and gendered (Princess Margaret Theresa under the gaze of a chaperone, dressed in mourning, talking to a dimly lit bodyguard). Furthermore, the revelation of these conditions translates into further sub-jectivities outside the frame—this reflexive doubleness subconsciously reveals to the viewer of the painting his or her own identity, a self-conscious Otherness that is spatial, three-dimensional, and simultaneously included and excluded from the frame of representation.

In several recent African American museums, the use of visual symbols to render cultural identity remains two-dimensional at best. For museums like the Reginald F. Lewis Museum of Maryland African American History and Culture in Baltimore (2005), the Center for Civil and Human Rights in

Atlanta (2012), and the New Africa Center in New York (2015), blackness is found in the colors of black liberation (red, yellow, and black, colors coincidentally also found in the Maryland state flag), façades of alternating shades of sandstone or limestone, or façade patterns inspired by African woven fabrics. The frequent references in this kind of architecture to woven fabrics are most often drawn from Ghanaian kente cloth, made by the Ashante people of Ghana and the Ewe people of Ghana and Togo—Africa's Gold Coast.

The paradox of kente cloth is that it has become immensely popular internationally as an indicator of black identity while only representing a limited range of African heritage. Only 14 percent of the slaves exported from Africa by the English and French between 1711 and 1810 were from the Gold Coast; far more came from areas like Nigeria (39.6 percent) and southwestern African countries like Cameroon and Angola (24.7 percent), representing twenty-five different ethnic groups in addition to the six major ethnic groups of the Gold Coast. Historically, Kente was a royal cloth, but it also appears in many other important forms of regalia among the Ashante and Ewe, including drums, shields, umbrellas, and fans. Over the past forty years, the cloth has been transformed into hats, ties, bags, and many other accessories worn and used on both sides of the Atlantic. Individual kente strips are especially popular in the United States where they are sewn into liturgical and academic robes or worn as a "stole." Kente patterns have developed a life of their own, appropriated as surface designs for everything from Band-Aids and balloons to beach balls and Bible covers.[10]

The lack of conceptual or visual depth in each of these building envelopes is an absence of what could possibly be more than skin deep. Since the avant-gardes of the early twentieth century, it has been understood that color might be employed as propaganda and that the spatial patterning of façade elements might strike a particular stance regarding industrial processes. But these more recent buildings do not recognize the political potency of image making, either for cultural advertisements or for critiquing an economic status quo based on commercialization and the consumption of images. Furthermore, they do not take explicit positions regarding the technological processes of building production and the history of black labor in America.

The National Civil Rights Museum at the Lorraine Motel in Memphis (1992), the Museum of the African Diaspora (MOAD) in San Francisco (2005), and the International Civil Rights Center and Museum in

Greensboro (2010), all exercise another trope of cultural representation in architecture—the use of photographic images to signify collective identity. In the case of MOAD, a mosaic of more than two thousand faces of people from around the world—illuminated behind the building's commercial storefront façade of the first three floors of the St. Regis Hotel and Towers—is meant to explore the ties of African-Americans to Africa. The mosaic was conceived of by the museum's graphic designer, Deborah Sussman, and its imagery is potent—but also a missed opportunity, in that the mosaic's representation of this diasporic connectivity does not engender the reconceptualization of the museum's architecture as being itself a container of that collection of identities.[11]

At the Lorraine Motel (the site of the assassination of Dr. Martin Luther King, Jr. in Memphis, Tennessee) and the International Civil Rights Center and Museum (the site of the heroic 1960 sit-in at the "whites only" F.W. Woolworth store lunch counter in Greensboro, North Carolina), the iconic photographs that mark the significance of each site challenge the architecture's ability to come to terms with the profundity of these events. Judge D'Army Bailey—the founder of the National Civil Rights Museum at the Lorraine Motel—said at the museum's opening that "the museum is a propaganda vehicle to create more soldiers and generals to carry on our fight for equality, by teaching them and showing them what we came through, who and what our leaders were. The major thrust of the museum is that the movement did not die in 1968, that others picked up Dr. King's work and carried on."[12] But throughout the article in which Bailey articulated this mission (in an April 1992 issue of *Ebony* magazine), the museum is alternately referred to as a shrine and a memorial. The emotional climax of the museum is the balcony on which Dr. King was shot, while the historical climax resides in Room 307, where Dr. King slept. As visitors enter Room 307 and the adjoining Room 306, a glass etching of Dr. King's likeness and recording of Mahalia Jackson singing "Precious Lord"—Dr. King's favorite song—plays as visitors pass through the narrow glass-walled passageway that separates the rooms.

Herein lies the struggle that the architecture of this and other museums fail to come to terms with. Is the museum a propaganda vehicle that projects forward, or is it a memorial? How should the museum respectfully honor Dr. King's memory while at the same time translate the memories of the Civil Rights movement into action? How should the motel be transformed to expose future potentialities and overcome the site's incredible weight of emotion and sentiment? That the exhibition sequence ends in Room 307 with a song of enormous emotional gravity—not only sung by Mahalia Jackson at civil rights rallies to inspire crowds, but also more often sung at funerals in African American churches—mires the architecture in this conundrum. The design of the museum should be challenged to construct a cultural discourse that probes deeper than the emotions that resonate on imagistic surfaces like the photos of the fallen Dr. King on the balcony of the Lorraine Motel.

Similarly, the famous photograph of four North Carolina Agricultural and Technical State University students passively challenging injustice and inequality throughout the South by refusing to leave their seats at the lunch counter in Greensboro challenges the architectural intervention at the International Civil Rights Center and Museum. The nonviolent sit-in was a radical act of defiance that exceeds the possibility of photographic representation. Civil rights protesters routinely faced mortal danger at the hands of law enforcement, whether in the form of water cannons, dogs, or arrest, and it was within this state of normalized violence that the "Greensboro Four"—Ezell Blair, Jr., David Richmond, Franklin McCain, and Joseph McNeil—staged the first sit-in on February 1, 1960. They broke Jim Crow laws, challenged the racist legal system, faced taunts and physical abuse by white patrons, and confronted the threat of being thrown in jail, or even the loss of their lives.

They took radical action to bring about radical change. In his discussion of the blues and its emphasis on the tragic struggles of African Americans, Cornel West links the heroic actions of ordinary people reacting to the radical contingencies of everyday life to a history of American pragmatism. This is a form of cultural awareness that is intimately tied to historical consciousness,

> always viewing oneself as embedded and embodied and also indebted to those who came before. So there is that sense of radical conditionedness on the one hand and, on the other, a sense of freedom, but still with that context of radical conditionedness, especially to oneself. There is the sense of trying to muster the courage to be oneself, the courage to wrestle with the truth about oneself, the truth about America, the truth about the world and the courage to fight for justice.[13]

Hence, the protesters' actions—in the context of radical conditioned-ness—were in fact acts of freedom. Therefore the problem for architecture and its expressions does not reside in the museum's objecthood or repre-sentational imagery, but rather in the ways that it enables action and event. As Foucault has observed, institutions and their architectural embodiments are never the guarantors of liberty, though they can at times open them-selves to the possibility of understanding that dichotomy between freedom and conditionedness. "Liberty," Foucault argues, "is a *practice*," and it is a practice that can, in certain forms, be cultivated through a different kind of museum.[14]

The cultural space of the Woolworth store transformed into a museum should not be about the artifacts and objects but about spatial praxes, the relationships among things that cannot be identified as proper objects but yet constitute a material presence, and how identity was performed in the 1960 sit-ins and future performances of identity.[15] The Woolworth store and the museum should be liberated to perform identity.

Yet another means of rendering cultural identity in African American museums over the past thirty years has been the use of certain iconic metaphors as signifiers of "Africa." Such metaphors include domes (hut), ziggurats (pyramid), stool (throne), crypt or vessel (tomb), and crown (head-dress). They are used with the hope that the implicit and explicit attributes of the objects will invest the buildings with positive connotations (cultural heritage, legitimacy, and value) and make them "recognizable" and more ac-ceptable to the general public than if they were rendered in the language of architectural abstraction. These metaphors are often implemented as figu-ration in the elevations of the buildings, or as plan elements without respect to a particular place or cultural context. They do not speak to politics, so-cio-spatial relationships, or even historical specificity. The California African American Museum in Los Angeles (1984), the Charles H. Wright Museum of African American History in Detroit (1997), and the newly planned National Museum of African American History and Culture in Washington, DC (projected to open in 2016) utilize these kinds of signifying metaphors.

The modest looking, low profile, horizontal California African American Museum (CAAM), with its somewhat diminutive scale, never had a chance of competing with its tall and extremely close neighbor, Frank Gehry's Aerospace Museum. As a meager attempt to establish an honorific pres-ence on its triangular site in Exposition Park, the museum's entry is defined by an apse-shaped portico with round columns supporting a concrete beam set against a ziggurat-shaped pediment. These entry elements do not produce real meaning, but rather are scenographic effects—a de-historicized architecture appended to a triangular modern building.

The Charles H. Wright Museum of African American History uses similar scenographic effects at its two main entrances to signify the honorific status of the museum. Poised above each entrance is a gold and black mask embellished with gold plated bands, diamond shapes, and rosettes designed by the sculptor Richard Bennett. The masks, called "Sentry," are modeled on N'tomo society masks from the Bambara people of Mali. Each mask consists of six horns, which have been described as an evocation of the anatomy of antelopes, linking animal and human forms.[16] But the Bambara masks are in fact used in rituals of initiation, and the six horns atop the mask represent the six clans or societies called "dyo" that are in charge of instructing the youngest members of the village. The Sentry masks are each framed by diagonal elements that resemble crossed Egyptian scepters, and are supported by columns said to be based on an "African" rope motif. A main feature of the museum is its rotunda, covered with a glass and steel dome, with a structural logic similar to that of a round African thatched hut. The clear glazing at the bottom of the dome, just above its drum, resembles a series of pointed arches. Yet the array of arches is neither structural nor intended to form pendentives that transfer the structural load of the dome to the circular base. Instead, the bottom of the circular array of arches recalls the bottom of a Sahelian nomadic tent structure, found to the north of the Sudanian savannah in Africa.

The design for the National Museum of African American History and Culture (NMAAHC) relies upon its association with the image of the tiered capitals of the caryatid veranda posts at the Ogoga's palace in Ikere, Nigeria. (This is not a distant historical reference—the capitals were carved from wood by Olowe of Ise, a Nigerian artist, in the early 1900s.)[17] At the Ikere palace, the inverted pyramidal capitals were situated on the heads of posts representing the king and queen, although other veranda posts carved by Olowe placed tiered capitals upon warrior and even servant figures. At the NMAAHC, the use of the tiered, inverted pyramid is intended to invoke an honorific status, as well as to recall African American church hats, once an iconic symbol of black women and their "Sunday Go To Meetin'" finest wear. Another possible reading could be found in the tiered columns's striking resemblance to Brancusi's "Infinite Column" of 1938, although there is some dispute as to the extent of the influence of African art on Brancusi's work. That there may be multiple references for use of the inverted pyramid at the NMAAHC does not undermine the central intention of the metaphor, which is meant to connote something recognizable, imageable, and somehow "African." This metaphor, however, inevitably relies on an architectural fragment that has been removed from its historical and cultural context—thus ironically becoming only self-referential.

Furthermore, the museum, sited at the foot of the Washington Monument, only timidly acknowledges its panoptic relationship to the events and government institutions that are woven in the shared landscape of black American identity and the National Mall—the executive order emancipating the slaves, the legislation of civil rights, the adjudication of laws affecting civil liberties and rights, and the Great March on Washington in 1963. That the surrounding icons of government institutions within this network of relations—in particular the White House and the U.S. Capitol—were constructed with black slave labor is not a part of any discourse concerning the site's strategy or the architectural design. Instead, the NMAAHC's square footprint seems to be more preoccupied with its platonic relationship to other museums on the National Mall, such as the triangular shape of the National Gallery of Art East Building by I.M. Pei and the circular form of the Hirshhorn Museum by Gordon Bunshaft.

The use of de-historicized architectural fragments that aspire to something recognizably "African," plainly visible at the CAAM, the Charles H. Wright Museum, and the NMAAHC, is marked with the scent of architectural postmodernism. The use of *modernist* architectural clichés in projects like the National Underground Railroad Freedom Center in Cincinnati (2004) and the August Wilson Center for African American Culture in Pittsburgh (2009) is no less suspect. At the Underground Railroad Freedom Center, curving pathways representing the winding paths to freedom of slaves on the Underground Railroad also define the curved walls of the museum's three linked pavilions, and that linkage is in turn intended to commemorate the cooperation of diverse groups that worked to overcome slavery. The museum is set on the north bank of the Ohio River, sandwiched between the Cincinnati Reds baseball stadium on one side and the Cincinnati Bengals football stadium on the other.

Cincinnati has a complex history in regards to civil liberties and civil rights. The city was one of the first stops on the Underground Railroad where slaves could not be recaptured and taken back across the river to southern slave states; it was in Cincinnati that police arrested Dennis

Barrie, director of the Contemporary Arts Center, on obscenity charges
when he exhibited homoerotically explicit photographs by Robert
Mapplethorpe in 1990; in that same decade, the owner of the Cincinnati
Reds, Marge Schott, referred to two black players with a racial slur and
made admiring public statements about Hitler; until 2002, the Ku Klux Klan
often displayed a cross during the Christmas holidays in Fountain Square;
and fifteen black men, including an unarmed teenager fleeing arrest, have
died in confrontations with the police between 1996 and 2001.[18] Despite
this profoundly charged urban context, the museum's symbolic curving
pathways stop at the building's property lines, and the architectural design
makes little attempt at relating to the fabric of the city. The three pavilions
with their curved walls sit as objects in a de-contextualized landscape, separated from the city by more than eight lanes of roadway and an interstate
underpass. The clichéd curves of the site and the pavilions frame the building as a neutral object, making the museum more like the entertainment
venues along the river—an unthreatening engine of redevelopment—than a
cultural institution.

The August Wilson Center for African American Culture in Pittsburgh
likewise relies on a symbolically curved wall, this time turned vertically
to resemble a three-story-tall sail. The height of the sail-like wall bestows
"iconic" status on the building. It does not mark the entry to the building;
rather, it is a visual marker intended to be part of the vista from a nearby
intersection. Nor does the three-story curved wall contain a significant public space or triple-height volume, as might be expected from its prominence
(and given its intention to invoke the memory of a slave ship as a shared
history for African American ancestors). The curved wall is very much a
façade, an image of a tall sail that is not only a cliché of contemporary ico-
nicity but also a cliché of modernist architecture, which considered ships
as emblems of modernity and industrialization. In Le Corbusier's chapter
on "Eyes Which Do Not See," from *Vers une architecture* (1923), images
of steamships and sailing vessels serve as examples of *l'esprit nouveau*
and encourage architects to pursue a kind of beauty of a more technical
order. Le Corbusier critiques the styles of the past as the surface decora-
tion of façades, arguing that "this is the degeneration of 'style.'"[19] But Le
Corbusier's metaphoric use of the steam liner itself became a cliché of the
high modernist period, and its relevance to a particular time and cultural
context was all but lost as the reference became subjected to its own representation as style.

An architectural cliché need not already exist in order for a design element or relationship between elements to become a cliché in the context of cultural identity. Such is the case of the competition-winning design for the Center for Civil and Human Rights in Atlanta, where the original design of the building was based upon the image of interlocking arms of civil rights marchers in the 1960s. This symbol of solidarity between people of diverse cultures and backgrounds is primarily represented in the plan outline of the building, and would have only been visible from the sky. The exhibition spaces in the design were located in one arm and the administrative functions in the other; this arrangement failed to yield a meaningful programmatic interlocking, and the public circulation begins at the space between the two *L's* rather than establishing a sequence that would begin at one *L* and flow to the next. Additionally, there is no differentiation between the two *L's* in terms of tectonics or materiality, diminishing the building's intended expression of the diversity within those interlocking figures. But such design decisions would be trivial anyway—the design was fundamentally not intended as a discourse on cultural diversity and its spatialization. Rather, the appropriation of shapes and imagery from famous photographs—even those that form much of our broadest cultural awareness of this historical moment—trivializes the radical acts of civil disobedience and the radical reshaping of socio-spatial relationships brought about by the Civil Rights Movement. Yet the "evolution" of the design into its final built form is even less conceptually ambitious. Opened in 2014, the building is primarily comprised of two curving walls leaning inward toward each other. In plan, the figure resembles a hut with openings at either end, while in section, it resembles a double lean-to structure. The curving walls are clad in alternating colored metal panels to resemble a woven African fabric.

Two particularly notable African American cultural institutions do not rely upon cultural stereotypes or architectural imagery steeped in metaphor and cliché, and these projects offer a way forward for a building type that will continue to be an important part of a larger project of cultivating black self-awareness. These are the Birmingham Civil Rights Institute (1993) and the Martin Luther King Jr. Center for Nonviolent Social Change in Atlanta (1984), both by the architect Max Bond, Jr.

The Birmingham Civil Rights Institute—an interpretive museum and research facility dedicated to human rights more generally—occupies a significant urban site bordering the 16th Street Baptist Church and the Kelly Ingram Park. The 16th Street Baptist Church is the first African American church in downtown Birmingham, and the site where a bomb killed four young girls attending Sunday School on September 15, 1963. Crowds gathered to protest this bombing in the nearby Ingram Park, a scene made famous with images of guard dogs unleashed on marchers. The design of the building acknowledges its relationship to the park by pulling back from the street wall to create a wide sidewalk and forming a public space at the corner of 16th Street, allowing a cross-axial view of the church. [31–33] Additionally, the public sequence through the building begins at an interior courtyard where the domed roof of the entrance hall echoes neighborhood churches, without overwhelming them, by establishing an independently iconic presence. The circulation builds through a sequence of exhibition spaces, and the building only reasserts its presence at the conclusion of the sequence where two windows bring light into the final gallery (where one window frames a view of the 16th Street Baptist Church and the other looks onto Kelly Ingram Park, reminding the visitor again of the histories that are deeply embedded on the site).

In Atlanta, an open courtyard with reflecting pool surrounded by a vaulted colonnade sets up a sequence of movement whereby the visitor is always aware of the space's relationship to the King Memorial, a sarcophagus faced with white Georgia marble inscribed with an epitaph taken from Dr. King's Mountaintop speech—"Free at last, free at last, thank God Almighty, I'm free at last"—set on a circular brick island in the center of the reflecting pool. While visitors are always aware of the memorial, they are never too close. The visitor's perception of the memorial (and of the memory of Dr. King more generally) are defined through specific perspectival views, reflections of the memorial itself, and the play of light and shadow between the surface of the pool and the darker interior surfaces of the vaulted colonnade. [34–36] The massing of the vaults and the forms of the various buildings create an interplay of solid and void, presence and absence, rather than relying on iconographic imagery or symbols.

The Birmingham Civil Rights Institute and the Martin Luther King, Jr. Center for Nonviolent Social Change are only two among the large number of African American cultural institutions designed and constructed over the last few decades that do not use cultural stereotypes to communicate cultural identity through design. Yet these two examples were constructed over twenty-five years ago. Hence the questions remain: Why does architecture continue to prop up and perpetuate African American stereotypes and "Africanisms" through imagery, metaphors, and clichés? Why do these cultural stereotypes persist? Even if these stereotypes are due to a long history of "othering" black Americans (largely by their white cousins, who remain loath to acknowledge their own indebtedness to African and African American culture): Why does architecture not interrogate this condition to produce architectural works of merit, instead of mythologizing the notion of "Africa" and using skin-deep aesthetics to assert legitimacy and to mark out a symbolic legacy?

In reference to the black film historian Thomas Cripps, Michelle Wallace's "Why Are There No Great Black Artists?" asserts that "we are in danger of getting wasted by ghosts ... by 'black shadows on the silver screen,' by effusions and visual trances that haunt us because we refuse to look them in the eye."[20] Perhaps we in the field of architecture refuse to look beyond these ghostly reflections in our own pupils. This lack of critical design and discourse—what Wallace calls "the visual void" in black discourse—ironically perpetuates black American invisibility in architectural design.

NOTES

1. W.E.B. Du Bois, "The Souls of Black Folk–of Our Spiritual Strivings," in *Writings* (New York: Literary Classics of the United States, 1986), 364–65.

2. Du Bois, "The Souls of Black Folk," 365. Du Bois states that "the history of the American Negro is the history of this strife–this longing to attain self-conscious manhood, to merge his double self into a better and truer self."

3. Bridget R. Cooks, *Exhibiting Blackness: African Americans and the American Art Museum* (Amherst: University of Massachusetts Press, 2011), 2–3.

4. See Jesse Holland, *Black Men Built the Capitol* (Guilford: Globe Pequot Press, 2007), 3–4. "One of the things that I found was that actual African American slaves were used in the construction of the U.S. Capitol and the White House. Out of just about the 600 or so people who worked on the Capitol, maybe about 400 were African American slaves… Most people look at the Statue of Freedom now and they think, this is the statue of an American Indian on top of the Capitol. No, it's not. It's actually a statue of a freed slave with an American eagle helmet on top."

5. Elisabeth Bronfen, *Over Her Dead Body: Death, Femininity, and the Aesthetic* (Manchester: Manchester University Press, 1992), 182.

6. Michael Pickering, *Stereotyping: The Politics of Representation* (Hampshire: Palgrave MacMillan, 2001), 3.

7. Cornel West, *Race Matters* (Boston: Beacon Press, 1993), 4.

8. Ann Geracimos, "About Dashikis and the New Breed Cat," *New York Times*, Report on Men's Wear (April 1969), 93 and 101.

9. Michel Foucault, "Las Meninas," in *The Order of Things: An Archaeology of the Human Sciences* (New York: Vintage Books, 1970), 8.

10. *Wrapped in Pride: Ghanaian Kente Cloth and African American Identity*, exhibition at the Smithsonian Museum National Museum of African Art (1999).

11. The mosaic behind the glass façade of the Museum of the African Diaspora in San Francisco–conceived by Deborah Sussman and composed by Robert Silvers of Runaway Technology–is based on a photograph of an African girl by Chester Higgins, Jr. The composite image pixellates more than 2,000 individual images. "Beyond Black + White," *Metropolis* (March 2006), 104.

12. "King Memorial: Memphis Motel Becomes a Shrine," *Ebony* (April 1992): 56.

13. Cornel West, *The Cornel West Reader* (New York: Civitas Books, 1999), 23–24. Cornel West sets the foundation for the link between the history of American pragmatism and how black Americans deal with radical contingencies and the struggle for justice in his 1993 essay, "Pragmatism and the Tragic," published in

Prophetic Thought in Postmodern Times (Monroe, ME: Common Courage Press, 1993), 31–32.

14. "So there may, in fact, always be a certain number of projects whose aim is to modify some constraints, to loosen, or even to break them, but none of these projects can, simply by its nature, assure that people will have liberty automatically, that it will be established by the project itself. The liberty of men is never assured by the institutions and laws that are intended to guarantee them. This is why almost all of these laws and institutions are quite capable of being turned around. Not because they are ambiguous, but simply because 'liberty' is what must be exercised....where liberty is effectively exercised, one would find that this is not owing to the order of objects, but, once again, owing to the practice of liberty." Michel Foucault, "Space, Knowledge, and Power," interview with Paul Rabinow, in *The Foucault Reader* (New York: Pantheon Books, 1984), 245–46.

15. In "On the Ontology of Events: A Conversation with Bernard Tschumi," Peter Macapia discusses the ontology of architecture around the problem of program and event rather than the problem of form, an ontology that Delueze discovered in the ancient Stoics and their interest in limits, mixtures, time, space, and events. Online at www.petermacapia.com/blog/conversationbernardtschumi (25 October 2008).

16. Dennis Alan Nawrocki, ed., *Art in Detroit Public Places* (Detroit: Wayne State University Press, 2008), 65.

17. A photograph taken by Eva L.R. Meyerowitz in 1937 (the year before Olowe died) and published in 1943 in her article "Wood-Carving in the Yoruba Country To-Day" illustrates the veranda post in situ. The exact year they were carved and installed is unknown. See Roslyn Adele Walker, "The Ikere Palace Veranda Posts by Olowe of Ise," *African Arts,* vol. 24, no. 1 (January 1991): 77–78 and 104.

18. Bruce Weber, "The Road to Freedom, Revisited," the *New York Times,* August 1, 2004.

19. See "Eyes Which Do Not See" in Le Corbusier, *Vers une architecture* (1923), reprinted as *Towards a New Architecture*, trans. Frederick Etchells (New York: Dover Publications, 1986), 90–103.

20. Michelle Wallace, "Why Are There No Great Black Artists? The Problem of Visuality in African American Culture," in *Dark Designs & Visual Culture* (Durham: Duke University Press, 2004), 191.

(BLACK) SEXUALITY AND SPACE:
THE BODY AND THE GAZE

A discourse on black subjectivity in contemporary architectural theory is virtually non-existent. Architecture historically privileges the construction of perspectival space through the gaze of the white male subject, from Pietro Perugino's *Christ Handing the Keys to St. Peter* (1481–83)—whose primary actors are represented as fair-skinned European men with Roman features (although Christ and the Apostles were from Palestine and likely of darker skin tones)—to Mies van der Rohe's perspective collages that unbind space in a manner that dislocates the stationary viewpoint and collapses it at the eye of the author. Within this spectrum, architectural space is conceptualized as a rational, linear system of spatial projection in which privileged and honorific bodies are captured within view and all other bodies and objects that lie beyond the cone of vision are excluded from the frame of the picture plane. In architectural representation, black bodies systematically fall beyond the frame of reference for spatial inclusion; likewise in architectural discourse, black bodies are either invisible, occupy unspoken spaces of colonial subjugation, or dismissed to locations of repressive difference where the black body is simultaneously an object of desire and derision, yet has no desires of its own.

The initial questions that come to mind ponder over the subjectivities that were relegated to the hidden kitchen entrances and rear doors of restaurants, hotels, and doctors' offices during the Jim Crow era; the subjectivities that occupy the servant positions within Modernism's hierarchal dyad of "served" and "servant" spaces; and the subjectivities of the curved, feminized, and "primitive" bodies to which Modernism refers as irrational, dangerous, and difficult, but which nevertheless signify sensuousness in contrast to the straight-lined rationality of the modernist grid. However, such considerations rarely occupy a position in architectural theory. Hence, black subjectivity is not just an "other" in modern architectural discourse; architectural theory represents a space of exclusion of black subjectivity.

The basis for that exclusion can be traced to Georg Wilhelm Friedrich Hegel's posthumously published *Lectures on the Philosophy of History,* presented at the University of Berlin in 1822, 1828, and 1830. According to Maurice Merleau-Ponty, "All the great philosophical ideas of the past century—the philosophies of Marx and Nietzsche, phenomenology, German existentialism, and psychoanalysis—had their beginnings in Hegel; it was he who started the attempt to explore the irrational and integrate it into an expanded reason which remains the task of our century."[1] In the *Lectures on the Philosophy of History*, Hegel presents his theory of a universe rooted in the idea that the civilizing process, understood through various forms of history, is a rational proceeding that seeks rational freedom, to which Hegel refers as man's spirit and existence. In addition to outlining the various types of history, Hegel (in alignment with the philosophical racism of David Hume and the scientific racism of the Enlightenment) conducts a geographical survey of the world and provides an analysis of the cultural and intellectual acuity of each continent's inhabitants. Michelle M. Wright, in *Becoming Black: Creating Identity in the African Diaspora*, points out that Hegel positions the "Negro" outside of analytical history through examples of intellectual, technological, and moral histories as well as cultural progress—all of which exclude the "Negro."[2] According to Hegel, "The peculiarly African character is difficult to comprehend, for the very reason that in reference to it, we must quite give up the principle which naturally accompanies all our ideas—the category of Universality...The Negro, as already observed, exhibits the natural man in his completely wild and untamed state."[3] Furthermore, following his exegeses of the Negro's want of reason and consciousness, his acceptance of slavery and inability to appreciate freedom, which leads to a contempt of humanity, and his inability to construct systems of social and political order, Hegel states:

> From these various traits it is manifest that want of self-control distinguishes the charter of the Negroes. This condition is capable of no development or culture, and we see them at this day, such have they always been. The only essential connection that has existed and continued between the Negroes and the Europeans is that of slavery...At this point we leave Africa, not to mention it again. For it is no historical part of the World; it has no movement or development to exhibit. Historical movements in it—that is in its northern part—belong to the Asiatic or European World.[4]

In the text, Hegel positions the Negro in counter-distinction to the white European and delineates this dichotomy to illustrate that not only does the Negro lack consciousness and therefore subjectivity but he is also driven by irrational thought processes and inhuman desires. On the other hand, the white European is motivated by rational thought processes evidenced by organized forms of political and social orders, scientific and technological achievements, and desire for progress. Yet the implicit paradox of this dialectic is that while Hegel positions the Negro as the antithesis of the white European and outside of history, the Negro's inferior position is necessary in order to define the white subject. Within Hegel's explicitly racist analysis, superiority is dependent on a position of inferiority. By extension and irony, the anterior questions regarding the suppressed subjectivities of architectural discourse and its dark spaces of exclusion are illuminated and given presence.

Building upon this Hegelian foundation, modern philosophy's subject is assumed to lay in the consciousness of white male patriarchy. Here, the confluence of philosophy and psychoanalysis exposes the sexual biases in both discourses, and as such was refuted by feminist thinkers such as Simone de Beauvoir. For example, Jacque Lacan's notion of the "mirror stage", which conceptualizes the formation of the "I", theorizes that a male infant will recognize his image in a mirror and differentiate between his own body and the persons and things around him. In his 1949 lecture titled "The Mirror Stage as Formative of the Function of the I as revealed in Psychoanalytic Experience," delivered at the 16th International Congress of Psychoanalysis, Lacan states, "Unable as yet to walk, or even to stand up, and held tightly as he is by some support, human or artificial (what, in France, we call a 'trotte-bébé'), he nevertheless overcomes, in a flutter of jubilant activity, the obstructions of his support and, fixing his attitude in a slightly leaning-forward position, in order to hold it in his gaze, brings back an instantaneous aspect of the image."[5] For Lacan, the formation of the male "I" is the precursor to the formation of subjectivity, which supersedes all other constructions of a subject.

> This jubilant assumption of his specular image by the child at the *infans* stage, still sunk in his motor incapacity and nursling dependence, would seem to exhibit in an exemplary situation the symbolic matrix in which the I is precipitated in a primordial form, before it is objectified in the dialectic of identification with the other, and before language restores to it, in the universal, its function as subject. [6]

Therefore Lacan's subject is presumably already marked by gender but before the entrance into language. Furthermore, at this stage the child's ability to recognize himself as "*I*" is akin to recognizing his image as other which induces a self-alienation.

Simone de Beauvoir refutes this male-centric position in *The Second Sex*, originally published in June 1949 as *Le deuxième sexe*, nearly simultaneous to Lacan's lecture. Beginning with an assessment of the status of women and drawing upon Hegel's concept of the *Other*, de Beauvoir writes "Humanity is male, and man defines woman, not in herself, but in relation to himself; she is not considered an autonomous being.... She is determined and differentiated in relation to man, while he is not in relation to her; she is the inessential in front of the essential. He is the Subject; he is the Absolute. She is the *Other*."[7] Yet de Beauvoir also exposes the Hegelian paradox and what she describes as Hegel's fundamental hostility to any other consciousness while at the same time relying upon the *Other* in order to posit itself as the subject. However, de Beauvoir's critique is not limited to the oppression of women, but extends to the othering of subjectivity based upon class and race and how the social and natural sciences have been used to construct dichotomies between the subject and the *Other* in terms of superiority versus inferiority.

> To prove women's inferiority, antifeminists began to draw not only, as before, on religion, philosophy, and theology but also on science: biology, experimental psychology, and so forth. At most they were willing to grant 'separate but equal status' to the other sex. That winning formula is most significant: it is exactly that formula the Jim Crow laws put into practice with regard to black Americans; this so-called egalitarian segregation served only to introduce the most extreme forms of discrimination. This convergence is in no way pure chance: whether it is race, caste, class, or sex reduced to an inferior condition, the justification process is the same.[8]

The Second Sex is often described as the feminist bible, as it established the foundation for post-modern discourses on the identity politics of the feminist movement. Furthermore, given the inherent intersections of race, class, and sex, de Beauvoir's exposition also helped set the groundwork for social and political art of the neo-avant-garde of the 1970s through mid 1990s, often in terms of two primary locations: the body and gaze.

Many feminist art practices of the 1970s, 1980s, and 1990s theorized the female body as the material translation of the abjection assigned to it by patriarchy. This is exemplified through pain or trauma inflicted upon the body in the performances of such artists as Hannah Wilke, Gina Pane, and Carolee Schneemann. Through exaggerated eroticization, Hannah Wilke performs her body as an object and solicits the male gaze while reversing the gaze back upon itself through the exposition of her own sub-jectivity. This is exemplified by her performance photograph series *So Help Me Hannah* from 1978, and in particular the photograph *What Does This Represent/What Do You Represent (Reinhart)* (1978–84) included in the same series. In the photographs from *So Help Me Hannah,* Wilke pres-ents herself in various nude poses in high heels holding a gun. The image is overlaid with texts quoted from mostly male philosophers (including Edmund Burke, Karl Marx, and Friedrich Nietzsche) and male artists includ-ing Daniel Buren and David Smith. According to Amelia Jones's analysis of Wilke's work in *Body Art/Performing the Subject*, "Wilke, like so many feminists of the period, projects herself forward in physical action, but also explicitly lays claim to her intellectual capacity as body/self."[9] In *What Does this Represent/What Do You Represent (Reinhart)*, Wilke sits in the corner of a room, naked, wearing high heels, dejected, and holding a gun. Strewn at her feet are toy guns and Mickey Mouse dolls. The words from the title, taken from the modernist painter and illustrator Ad Reinhardt, are printed at the bottom of the photograph. Jones states that the abrupt, polemical nature of the text is intended "to disrupt any comfortable objecti-fication of Wilke as image; they also point to the way in which the rhetoric of aesthetics has been deployed at the expense of women, whose bodies are usually the unspoken objects of representation…Wilke's appropriation of Reinhart's statement reconfigures it towards a feminist critique."[10]

The feminist critique in Gina Pane's 1971 performance "Norriture, actualités televises, feu" reflects the artist's position that traditional rep-resentations of male projections onto the female body are insufficiently challenged by "positive" images of the female body, thus requiring a means by which the artist could confound conventional understandings of the body and rearticulate its status among patriarchy. The work, originally per-formed in 1971 in a Paris apartment, is divided into three parts, staging the body at intersections of gender, violence, and representation in a man-ner recalling the transgressive surrealisms of Georges Bataille. "Pane began by devouring a large quantity of raw ground meat followed by spitting it out again. In the second sequence, Pane sat with other partici-pants watching the evening news, while she was dazzled by a bright light coming from a lamp that was directed towards her eyes. In the last section, she tried to extinguish a fire ignited on a small hill of sand using her bare hands and feet."[11] In contrast to conventional representations of the female body as a hopeful symbol of salvation in a time of violence, war, and de-struction, Pane's body is intended as a catalytic agent to collapse the distance between foreground and background, between the partici-pants and the suffering and pain viewed on the evening news.

Similarly, in "Interior Scroll" Carolee Schneemann dislocates traditional gendered subjectivity. In "Interior Scroll", originally performed in 1975, Schneemann insinuates the hyper-sexualized objectification of the female body, and in particular female genitalia, by "pulling a long, thin coil of paper from her vagina ('like a ticker tape… plumb line… the umbilicus and tongue') unrolling it to read a narrative text to the audience. Part of this text read as follows: 'I met a happy man, / a structuralist filmmaker … he said we are fond of you / you are charming / but don't ask us / to look at your films / … we cannot look at / the personal clutter / the persistence of feelings / the hand touch sensibility.'"[12] Schneeman simultaneously recon-stitutes her own subjectivity while confounding the patriarchal white male gaze between the poles of desire and identity.

Yet like the Hegelian paradox that requires the Negro's position of inferiority in order to establish the white male's position of superiority and thereby delineate the white male's subjectivity, the white male gaze must maintain a privileged status for the white female body even though his objectifying gaze works to suppress white female subjectivity. That privi-leged status is necessary to the inferiority of the black female body for the sake of his own European based narcissism within Hegel's geographic ordering of history, reason, and rationalism, and by reason of his own hi-erarchy at the originating point of perception and a universal ordering of knowledge, as exemplified by Leonardo da Vinci's *Vitruvian Man*. The white male body is the center of a universal circle that occludes the black body to the invisible margins.

But if the Negro in Hegel's description has no historical part in the world and is cast somewhere Other, then the black female body in relationship to the white female body is "by virtue of color and feature and the extreme metaphors of enslavement…at the outermost reaches of 'otherness' … she subsumes all the roles of the not-white body."[13] This description comes

from Lorraine O'Grady's analysis of Édouard Manet's painting *Olympia*
from 1863, in an essay titled "Olympia's Maid: Reclaiming Black Female
Subjectivity." O'Grady points out that the black servant, modeled by a
professional named Laura, is a peripheral Negro who is intended to dis-
appear into the background drapery. In contrast to the figure of Olympia
posed nude upon the bed, Laura's place is outside of what can be conceived of as woman. Hence, the construct of relationships between black
and white bodies and subjectivities might be best described by a matrix
that positions the European (white male) subject at the upper left quadrant, the white female body in the adjacent upper right quadrant, the Negro
(non-subject) in the lower left quadrant below the European (white male)
subject, but in direct relationship in order to establish the European's superiority, and the black female body (non-subject) at the infinite limits of the
lower right quadrant—removed from view but necessarily present in order to
lend stability to the construct's hierarchical order.

   Sander L. Gilman's analysis of Manet's *Olympia* in "Black Bodies,
White Bodies: Toward an Iconography of Female Sexuality in Late
Nineteenth Century Art, Medicine, and Literature" notes that the black
servant signifies the sexuality of the central figure, and in other works of
art serves as a marker for the presence of illicit sexual activity. The obvi-
ous reference in this analysis is to Saartjie Baartman, better known as the
"Hottentot Venus," whose naked body was exhibited in London and Paris
from 1810 to 1815 and whose physical appearance became an icon of
sexual difference in Europe in the nineteenth century. However, the black
female body in the analysis still lacks subjectivity and remains a merely ob-
jectified marker of difference and deviance.[14] Yet the black female body
does occupy a space within the matrix of subjectivities and bodies, and
as such, its spatial praxes, whether visible or invisible, yield its poten-
tial agency to reference its own self rather than to focus on exposing the
hidden contradictions and assumptions of white male dominant hierarchy. Hence, we are confronted with the question of how to reassess these
spatial praxes in order to reclaim the body as a site for black female subjectivity, and to claim a space for black subjectivity in spatial discourse and
architectural theory.

A little more than a century after the exhibition of the "Hottentot Venus,"
race and sex intersected with spatial praxes and architectural theory in two

projects for modernist houses. One was the house for Josephine Baker designed by Adolf Loos in Paris in 1928, which became a celebrated and frequently discussed contribution to the European canon; the other, barely known to most architects, was the house named Azurest South, designed by an unknown, self-taught black female architect named Amaza Lee Meredith for herself and her life-long female companion in Petersburg, Virginia in 1939. In certain analyses, Josephine Baker, whose art is exposure, epitomizes the European history of ethnographic representations and the racist and sexist history of the objectification and desire of European Primitivism, similar to the "Hottentot Venus". According to historian Farès el Dahdah in "The Josephine Baker House: For Loos's Pleasure," the house reflects a desire to see and to touch her eroticized nude body, bathed in the light while swimming in an elevated enclosed indoor pool that Baker could access from her boudoir.[15] The house is about the theatrical spectacle of Josephine Baker and its design exemplifies the racial and sexual desires of European white male Modernist Primitivism.

On the other hand, Amaza Lee Meredith, a college professor, artist, and arts educator, is the anti-thesis of exposure with an unassuming presence—perhaps due to the nature of her personal relationship, which was unspoken of at the time, as well as the fact that she was one of the first black female architects in the United States practicing in a profession dominated by white males. However, Meredith's Azurest South is simultaneously a bold statement of belief in the doctrines of Modern architecture and a re-scripting its masculinist codes. Although the main body of the house exists on one level, its exterior shares certain semblances with the masked exterior of Loos's Villa Müller, designed in 1928. [37] In fact, Meredith's annotation on a photograph in her archives refers to the studio in the house (where she kept her library and art materials) as "My Lady's Boudoir," which is a clear reference to the withdrawn and inwardly facing *Damenzimmer* (lady's room/boudoir) of Villa Müller and a recoding of male authorship and authority.

In contrast to the introverted spaces of Loos and Meredith's boudoirs, Josephine Baker's art of exposure and its visual complexities began on October 2, 1925 when "La Revue Négre" opened at the Théâtre des Champs-Elysées and Baker crawled onto the stage with her mouth painted in minstrel style, wearing cut-off pants and a frayed shirt, accompanied by other dancers dressed as black "mammies" and "bucks," and performed a feverish version of the Charleston. She returned to the stage that evening

for her second appearance and closing routine of the show and performed
Danse Sauvage. Wearing only pink feathers around her waist, ankles
and neck, Baker's bare-chested body was splayed out and hung upside
down upon the back of her male black dance partner, Joe Alex, who was
equally naked except for beads around his neck, wrists, and ankles. The
performance elicited thunderous applause as well as shock and disgust. It
was the hit of show and launched Baker's European career.

However, Baker's early career as a vaudeville performer in New York
was not only an escape from poverty and the suppression she had experienced as a live-in domestic worker for white families in St. Louis, but it was
also the beginning of her own agency towards constructing a visibility that
would simultaneously beguile and vex European audiences. And although
she was cast in "La Revue Négre" by French producers who had come to
New York in search of an all black cast for a musical review in Paris, Baker's
energetic and spectacular performances far surpassed audience expecta-
tions and her role as an entertainer. Instead, these performance – along with
Baker's infamous "banana dance," in which she wore multi-strand beaded
necklace and a skirt made of a single string of bananas (that at once carry
phallic, racial, and colonial insinuations) – yield a complex and ambiguous
set of questions regarding the sensuous space between agency, performance, and spectacle. Baker's beads, feathers, and bananas not only
supplement the sensuality of her presentation, but these ornamentations
also signify Baker's self-fetishization that works to confound relationships
between subject, object, and desire.

Ironically, sensuousness and sensuality have always seemed anathema
and gratuitous to modern architecture and theory, known more for its func-
tionalist dogmas and Puritan attitudes towards program and typologies,
rationality, and structural order. In "Ornament and Crime," Loos excoriates
the criminality of ornament and sensuous dress, stating that those who go
around in velvet jackets are not artists but clowns or house painters and
that he (Loos) preaches to "the person at the peak of humanity, who yet
has a profound understanding of the problems and aspirations of those at
the bottom." Furthermore, in the same discriminating voice, Loos states:

> I can accept the ornament of the African, the Persian, the
> Slovak peasant woman, my shoemaker, because they have
> no other means to achieve elevated states of being. We,
> on the other hand, possess the art that has superseded

ornament. After the trials and tribulations of the day, we can
go hear Beethoven or Tristan. My shoemaker can't do that.
I can't take away his joy because I have nothing to replace it
with. But anyone who goes to hear the Ninth Symphony
and then sits down to design a wallpaper pattern is either a
criminal or a degenerate.[16]

Loos's statement appears to indirectly echo Hegel's statements regarding
the Negro's inferiority, and the claim that the Negro is incapable of cultural
development. Architectural historian Christopher Long, in "The Origins
and Context of Adolf Loos's 'Ornament and Crime,'" points out that the
foundation for Loos's statements about the path of cultural development was probably based upon the writings of Max Nordau, a preeminent
European political and social journalist who had been based in Paris
and who contributed to the Vienna Neue Freie Press, the Berlin *Vossische
Zeitung*, and other Central European newspapers. Nordau's book
Entartung (Degeneration, 1892), "which had sounded a fierce critique
of modernism, was widely read throughout Europe at the turn of the century
and unleashed a fervid controversy about the nature and qualities of the
new trends in literature and painting."[17] Long seeks to give Loos cover from
later critiques by Reyner Banham and others who criticized his cursory
appropriations from texts such as Nordau's, as well as the reasonableness
of his argument, by stating:

Loos's argument about the evolution of ornament may indeed
be erected on a flimsy theoretical foundation, but he never
an attempted to posit a scholarly case; his essay was a
cultural inquiry and part of a more open dialogue. He intended
from the outset to entertain his audience, castigate his oppo-
nents, and establish his positions. "Ornament and Crime," like
all of Loos's essays, was intensely personal and subjective;
he sought to reach his audience through an appeal to what he
thought was common sense.[18]

However, perhaps it is for the exceptions Loos articulated in "Ornament
and Crime" that he supposedly accepted the commission to design
a house for Josephine Baker, for Loos was only one of a number of
avant-gardist artist to be seduced by Baker's presence. According to

various accounts, her circle included Jean Cocteau, Pablo Picasso, Fernand Léger, Ernest Hemingway, and Mies van der Rohe among others. Additionally, José Miguel Covarrubias designed costumes for her; Henri Matisse made a life-size cutout of her; Alexander Calder made a wire sculpture of her; Le Corbusier wrote of her in his diary and made sketches; and she posed for Man Ray. Accounts of Loos' relationship with Baker are vague and mostly second hand, coming from Claire Loos's biography *Adolf Loos Privat*, which quotes Loos's description of his first encounter with Baker, and from Kurt Unger, Loos's student and collaborator, who mentions the design in a letter to Ludwig Münz dated 23 July 1935. Ironically, Baker herself never mentions Loos or the design for the house in any of her memoirs or letters. The paradox of these circumstances, together with Loos's articulated position regarding ornament and his fascination with Baker, point towards the tensions inherent in Baker's performance of her self-construction and self-representation and the elusive question of agency versus spectacle. Baker's incessant self-fetishization simultaneously elicits the desire of the male hierarchical gaze while eluding its capture within a complex set of spatial relationships between sex, race, colonialism, and fantasy. In "What Bananas Say" from *Second Skin: Josephine Baker and the Modern Surface,* Anne Anlin Cheng's analysis of Baker's destabilizing effects upon the translation between racial and sexual fetishism points to the resulting aspects of a conjunction between race and sexuality, particular in Baker's banana dance routine. Cheng states,

> Instead of establishing a clear-cut dichotomy between viewer and view, subject and object, master and slave, the mise-en-scène actually enables and encapsulates a complex network of mediated desires and cross-narratives. If we see the Baker-banana-Alex collaboration as a fantasy tableau, the viewer's entry point into it is significantly multiple. This suggests that the pleasures of racial fetishism for the fetishist (be that the master or the slave) are not that they protect one from racial otherness, but that they launch one into an imaginary scenario where one gets to *have* and *be* that otherness.[19]

Despite certain critiques that suggest the house Loos designed for Baker epitomizes a European white male, and possibly Loos's own, masculinist and Primitivist racial and sexual desires, the house – similar to Baker's performances – can be seen to contain similar ambiguities between viewer and view and subject and object. The house not only signifies the objectification of Baker but also her elusiveness and the illusiveness of her image within liminal conditions that flirt back and forth between two perceptual poles, ultimately rendering Baker's body unattainable.

These ambiguities begin at the exterior of the house, not in terms of its striped façade of alternating black and white stone, but in terms of the windows that present framed views from the interior towards Parisian street life, as well as framed views from the exterior for passersby secretly desiring glimpses of Baker's body. [38] The ambiguities extend from the large scaled windows along the exterior to the salon and the peep show scaled windows at the passage adjacent to the elevated swimming pool. At the entrance to the house the viewer gazes up and expects to see Baker making a grand and theatrical descent on the monumental stairs. At the same moment, the viewer imagines Baker's awareness of the viewer and the possibility of the visual exchange. Distances in the house are designed to fix the gaze of the viewer upon the movement of Baker's body in space, and to induce an acknowledgement or at least an awareness of her admirers. Furthermore, on the *étage noble* and further along the public route of the house, the viewer imagines the possibility of being seen by Baker before seeing her. [39, 40]

In Lacan's lecture titled "The Place, Origin and End of My Teaching", presented at Vinatier in Lyon following the publication of *Ecrits*, Lacan states, "….desire full stop is always the desire of the *Other*. Which basically means that we are always asking the *Other* what he desires." In his full explanation of this statement, he explains that desire is fundamentally the desire for recognition by the Other and that these desires are repetitive and engaged in a transference: "The necessary and sufficient reason for the repetitive insistence of these desires in the transference and their permanent remembrance in a signifier that repression has appropriated – that is, in which the repressed returns – is found if one accepts the idea that in these determinations the desire for recognition dominates the desire that is to be recognized, preserving it as such until it is recognized." Furthermore, Lacan introduces a graph of desire found in his paper titled "The Subversion of the Subject and the Dialectic of Desire," and explains

> But we must also add that man's desire is the Other's desire (*le désir de l'homme est le désir de l'Autre*) in which the

> *de* provides what grammarians call a "subjective determina-
> tion"—namely, that it is qua Other that man desires (this is
> what provides the true scope of human passion).

> This is why the Other's question *(la question* de *l'Autre)*—that
> comes back to the subject from the place from which he ex-
> pects an oracular reply—which takes some such form as *"Che
> vuoi?,"* "What do you want?," is the question that best leads
> the subject to the path of his own desire, assuming that,
> thanks to the know-how of a partner known as a psychoana-
> lyst, he takes up that question, even without knowing it,
> in the following form: "What does he want from me?"[20]

In the house, the desire for Baker is actually the viewer's desire for himself to be desired by Baker, and Baker's elusiveness only works to heighten
those desires. The denouement of the viewer's experience of the Baker
House is the elevated, enclosed indoor swimming pool. The pool contains
windows along the side passage where the viewer can gaze at Baker's
body floating in water, and illuminated by daylight from the skylights above
the pool, as if in a dream or fantasy. However, the windows onto the swimming pool mirror windows along the exterior wall of the passage, which are
behind the viewer. Therefore, the viewer also sees his own image reflected
in the glass of the swimming pool windows enmeshed with the image of
Baker's body. Hence, the consciousness of the white male child in Lacan's
illustration of the "Mirror Stage" is foiled by the black female body. The hierarchical relationships and distance between subject and object collapse
in the picture plane of the swimming pool window.

Amaza Lee Meredith's Azurest South also works to confound the
hierarchical male gaze and its subject and object relationships. However,
the house subverts these relationships through the masculine guises
of Modernism while never yielding the agency of the black female bodies
of its inhabitants—Ms. Meredith and Dr. Edna Meade Colson. [41] The U.S.
National Register for Historic Places catalogues the many "International
Style" tropes contained in the house, which they describe as

> a "machine for living," devoid of applied ornament or his-
> toric references. Characteristic of the style, Azurest South
> has clean lines and a strong geometry emphasizing regularity

rather than symmetry. [42] The walls are concrete block fin-
ished in white stucco. The flat roof, designed as a terrace, is
highlighted by plain metal coping and by steel pipe rails
all painted a bright turquoise blue... A dominant feature of
the exterior is the bedroom wing whose curved corners are
articulated with horizontal ribbon windows of glass block.
A glass-block sidelight at the front door illuminates the coat
closet. Glass-block sidelights in the living room window are
echoed in the window centered in the shower wall. [43] A
single band of glass-block was positioned above the day bed
in the first studio.... The east elevation, overlooking the creek,
is dominated by a large, single-pane, square window light-
ing the living room. The roof terrace above, defined by its blue
pipe railing, provides outdoor living space.[21]

The language of European white male Modernism is clearly recognized
in this description. Its description as "devoid" of ornament or historic
references suggests that it is lacking that which would be expected. In
other words, the house is lacking any identifiable markers of domesticity
associated with sex or race. Considering the geographical and cultural context of the house (not far from the capital of the Confederacy during the
U.S. Civil War and constructed during the enforcement of Jim Crow laws
throughout the South, as well as the peak of Colonial Revival architecture
in Virginia), it displays no signs of female domesticity or of a black domestic
servant. Instead the house subverts representation and patriarchal power
structures through a "reverse othering" and its unexpectedness engages in
queering European white male Modernism. Audre Lorde notes in her text
"Age, Race, Class and Sex: Women Redefining Difference" that "in order
to survive, those of us for whom oppression is as American as apple pie
have always had to be watchers, to become familiar with the language and
manners of the oppressor, even sometimes adopting them for some illusion
of protection."[22]
 Amaza Lee Meredith was born in Lynchburg, Virginia and studied at
the Virginia Normal and Industrial Institute, now known as Virginia State
University. Following this, she taught mathematics in Lynchburg before mov-
ing to Brooklyn, New York in 1926 and enrolling at the Teachers College
of Columbia University during the Harlem Renaissance. She majored in fine
arts and received a bachelor's degree with honors in 1930 before

returning to Virginia State University to teach. She then took a brief leave of absence to return to Teachers College where she earned a master's degree in 1934. The details of her life in New York are unknown, however she did travel between Virginia and New York following the completion of her studies at Teacher's College to attend museums and cultural events. It is conceivable that Meredith may have returned to New York in 1935 for one of the lectures given by Le Corbusier at area architecture schools including Columbia University. She did, in fact, return to New York in 1936 for the opening of the "House of the Modern Age" at Park Avenue and East 39th Street, and she retained the entry ticket to the opening as a souvenir of the event. The house, designed by William Van Alen for National Houses Inc., was constructed of steel panels for ten thousand dollars as an experimental demonstration of modernist architecture and fabrication techniques. The two-story, eight-room building was covered in a stucco-like finish and included a patio, sun terrace, and built in garage. The International Style house was completely furnished with state-of-the-art appliances and modernist furniture to illustrate a modern aesthetic and lifestyle that with few exceptions had not yet taken hold in domestic architecture in the United States. Furthermore, the catalog for the exhibition illustrates the interior as replete with all the finishes for the modern domestic housewife, including wallpaper, fur carpeting, and plush lounge chairs.

The interior of Meredith's Azurest South exhibits a similar modernist aesthetic and is described as having been "enlivened by the vivid colors of the walls, floors, and ceilings" and a combination of contemporary and traditional materials in contrast to house's exterior severity.[23] Throughout the house, different surfaces of colored glass and tile, as well as colored geometric patterns and colored surfaces, allude to Meredith's vocation as a painter. [44] The living room, kitchen, and studio are relatively open spaces. A small vestibule separates the living room from the two bedrooms of Ms. Meredith and Dr. Colson that mirror each other, and are defined by a curved exterior wall with symmetrical windows and curved glass block at the building's south elevation. [45, 46] The exterior wall, with its small-scaled windows relative to the curved surface, acts as a mask that confounds the reading of the domestic interior and spatial relationships between its inhabitants. Furthermore, Meredith's isometric section and elevation drawings of the house pertain more to the technical aspects of its construction than to traditional ideas of gender in domestic architecture.

[47] A wall section reveals unadorned ceilings and walls lacking mouldings or trim. Neither race, sex, or sexuality is visible; yet, their re-codings are in plain sight.[24]

Returning to "Olympia's Maid," Lorraine O'Grady states that the question of modernism's demise must be left open as an option for the reclamation of black female subjectivity in feminist and visual theory. "For one thing, there seems no way around the fact that the method of reclaiming subjectivity precisely mirrors modernism's description of the artistic process. Whatever else it may require, it needs an act of will to project the inside onto the outside long enough to see and take possession of it," states O'Grady.[25] The question might also be put to architectural theory in terms of claiming a space for black subjectivity in architectural and spatial discourse. Yet, although black subjectivity may be relegated to the infinite limits of architecture's picture plane, its presence has historically been required in order to structure the center point of its narcissistic perspective view. Therefore O'Grady's question might be restructured in terms of projecting the outside to the inside of the frame of the picture plane—not in order to occupy the center but rather to excavate the ambiguous network of relationships that flicker back and forth for new terms that are no longer racially exclusive, but rather racially elusive and illusive.

NOTES

1. Maurice Merleau-Ponty, *Sense and Non-Sense*, trans. Hubert L. Dreyfus and Patricia Allen Dreyfus (Evanston: Northwestern University Press, 1964), 63.

2 Michelle M. Wright, *Becoming Black: Creating Identity in the African Diaspora* (Durham: Duke University Press, 2004), 8–29.

3. Georg Wilhelm Friedrich Hegel, *The Philosophy of History*, trans. J. Sibree (Kitchener: Batoche Books, 2001), 111.

4. Hegel, *The Philosophy of History*, 116–17.

5. Jacques Lacan, "The mirror stage as formative of the function of the I as revealed in psychoanalytic experience," *Écrits: A Selection,* trans. Alan Sheridan (New York: W.W. Norton & Company, 1977), 1.

6. Lacan, *Écrits,* 2.

7. Simone de Beauvoir, *The Second Sex,* trans. Constance Borde and Sheila Malovany-Chevallier (New York: Vintage Books, 2011), 26.

8. De Beauvoir, *The Second Sex*, 32.

9. Amelia Jones, *Body Art / Performing the Subject* (Minneapolis: University of Minnesota Press, 1998), 157.

10. Jones, *Body Art / Performing the Subject*, 157.

11. Anja Zimmermann, "'Sorry for Having to Make You Suffer': Body, Spectator, and the Gaze in the Performances of Yves Klein, Gina Pane, and Orlan," *Discourse,* vol. 24, no. 3 (Fall 2002), 32.

12. Jones, *Body Art / Performing the Subject*, 5.

13. Lorraine O'Grady, "Olympia's Maid: Reclaiming Black Female Subjectivity," *The Feminism and Visual Culture Reader*, ed. by Amelia Jones (New York: Routledge, 2003), 208.

14. See Sander L. Gilman, "Black Bodies, White Bodies: Toward an Iconography of Female Sexuality in Late Nineteenth-Century Art, Medicine, and Literature," *The Feminism and Visual Culture Reader*, ed. by Amelia Jones (New York: Routledge, 2003) for a discussion of the sexualized woman and the black woman traced from Monet, Richard Strauss, and William Hogarth to J.J. Virey's summary of the sexual nature of black females, and George Cuvier's post mortem of Saartjie Baartman's body including detailed examinations of her sexual genitalia and buttocks.

15. Farès el Dahdah, "The Josephine Baker House: For Loos's Pleasure," *Assemblage* 26 (April 1995), 75.

16. Adolf Loos, "Ornament und Verbrechen," *Adolf Loos, Trotzdem 1900–1930* (Innsbruck: Brenner, 1931), 93.

17. Christopher Long, "The Origins and Context of Adolf Loos's 'Ornament and Crime,'" *Journal of the Society of Architectural Historians*, vol. 68, no. 2 (June 2009): 208.

18. Long, "The Origins and Context of Adolf Loos's 'Ornament and Crime,'" 209.

19. Anne Anlin Cheng, *Second Skin: Josephine Baker and the Modern Surface* (Oxford: Oxford University Press, 2011), 46–47.

20. Jacques Lacan, "The Subversion of the Subject and the Dialectic of Desire," *Écrits,* trans. Bruce Fink (New York: W.W. Norton & Company, 2006), 690.

21. *Azurest South, Chesterfield County, Virginia*, National Register of Historic Places, Virginia Department of Historic Resources No. 020-5583, NRHP Registration (December 30, 1993), Section 7: 1.

22. Audre Lorde, "Age, Race, Class, and Sex: Women Redefining Difference," in *Sister Outsider: Essays and Speeches* (Trumansburg, NY: Crossing Press, 1984), 114.

23. *Azurest South, Chesterfield County, Virginia*, National Register of Historic Places, Section 7: 2–3.

24. Background information provided to the National Register of Historic Places states the following: "When Miss Meredith created Azurest South, she was a middle-aged woman who had established a small architectural practice, designing houses and interiors for family and friends. Little of her work is documented; her drawings are not those of a practiced architect, but rather those of a person who was familiar with both traditional and current trends in architectural design. She designed a house in Lynchburg for one sister and a residence in Sag Harbor for another sister. It is likely that the largest assemblage of her architectural projects can be found at Sag Harbor on Long Island. At Sag Harbor, a resort for wealthy whites, including the Roosevelt family, Miss Meredith and her family and friends created Azurest North, an enclave of vacation homes for middle-class blacks. Miss Meredith worked on design commissions at Sag Harbor into the 1970s when she was an elderly woman." Additionally, Meredith is known to have designed a house near Prairie View, Texas and another house near the campus of Virginia State University.

25. O'Grady, "Olympia's Maid: Reclaiming Black Female Subjectivity," 217.

CREDITS

BIOGRAPHY

Mario Gooden is a principal of Huff + Gooden Architects and a Professor of Practice at the Graduate School of Architecture, Planning and Preservation (GSAPP) of Columbia University where is also the co-Director of the Global Africa Lab (GAL). He is a 2012 National Endowment for the Arts Fellow and a MacDowell Colony Fellow.

ACKNOWLEDGEMENTS

Special thanks for their support, guidance, and inspiration

The late J. Max Bond

Amale Andraos
Luke Bulman
Beatriz Colomina
James Graham
Paul Gunther
Laurie Hawkinson
David Hinkle
Steven Holl
Ray Huff
Ryan King
Hilary Sample
Joel Sanders
Bernard Tschumi
Mark Wigley
Deborah Willis
Mabel Wilson

Drawings and Archives, Avery Architectural and Fine Arts Library
New York University Fales Library and Special Collections
Virginia State University Special Collections and Archives

Columbia University Office of the Vice Provost for Faculty Diversity and Inclusion
The MacDowell Colony
The National Endowment for the Arts

Columbia Books on Architecture and the City
An imprint of The Graduate School of Architecture, Planning and Preservation
Columbia University
407 Avery Hall
1172 Amsterdam Avenue
New York, NY   10027
Visit our website at www.arch.columbia.edu/books

Columbia Books on Architecture and the City are distributed by Columbia University Press
at cup.columbia.edu

All rights reserved
ISBN 978-1-941332-13-9

This book has been produced through the Office of the Dean, Amale Andraos and the Office of Publications
at Columbia University GSAPP.

Director of Publications: Isabelle Kirkham-Lewitt
Associate Editor: Joanna Joseph

Designer: Luke Bulman—Office with Camille Sacha Salvador
Copyeditor: Melissa Constantine
Image Editor: Ryan King
Printer: Regal Printing Limited

Library of Congress Cataloging-in-Publication Data

Names: Gooden, Mario, author.
Title: Dark space : architecture, representation, black identity / Mario
    Gooden.
Description: New York : Columbia Books on Architecture and the City, 2016. |
    Includes bibliographical references and index.
Identifiers: LCCN 2015045159 | ISBN 9781941332139 (alk. paper)
Subjects: LCSH: Architecture and race—United States. | African
    Americans—Race identity. | Architecture and society—United States.
Classification: LCC NA2543.R37 G66 2016 | DDC 720.89/96073—dc23
LC record available at http://lccn.loc.gov/2015045159

10 9 8 7 6 5 4 3